SPIRITUAL DEVELOPMENT
OF ST PAUL

SPIRITUAL DEVELOPMENT
OF ST PAUL

BY THE

REV. GEORGE MATHESON

M.A., D.D., F.R.S.E.

MINISTER OF THE PARISH OF ST BERNARD'S, EDINBURGH

NEW YORK
ANSON D. F. RANDOLPH AND CO.

EDINBURGH AND LONDON
WILLIAM BLACKWOOD AND SONS

MDCCCXCII

PREFACE.

THIS little book has occupied me at intervals nearly two years in writing, and a good many years in thinking. The problem I set before myself was this: assuming that the thirteen epistles of St Paul are genuine, and waiving for the present all questions of Biblical criticism, is it possible to regard these as marking the stages of a progressive development? Is it possible out of these alone, and without the aid of any foreign materials, to construct a fairly correct picture of the successive phases of Paul's Christian experience? The design of the book is therefore a limited one; it is strictly confined within these thirteen epistles. Even within these boundaries its title involves an additional limit. On the one hand it is a development of St Paul, not of Saul of Tarsus; on the other hand, it is his spiritual development, as distinguished alike from the course of his outer life and the growth of his intellectual system. I leave on the one side his missions, his shipwrecks, his dangers; I leave on the other his theology, whether as interpreted by the school of Tübingen or the school of Calvin, the discussion of Jewish or Gentile tendencies, of grace and law, of Episcopacy and Presbyterianism, of predestination and free-will. The only doctrines alluded to are those which bear upon the main thesis—the growth of his humanitarian consciousness, the widening of his sympathy from Jerusalem to Rome. The work, as will be seen from its dimensions, is merely the introduction to a vast subject. It indicates lines of development which might be followed out to any extent, but it has left it for others to do so. The authorities are the epistles themselves, and there is no citation from any German or English work. I have studied above all things to keep the mind not only unbiassed by, but as much as possible forgetful of, previous speculations, and have striven to gather the materials only from what claims to be the original source.

GEORGE MATHESON.

19 St Bernard's Crescent,
 Edinburgh, 1890.

CONTENTS.

SPIRITUAL DEVELOPMENT OF ST PAUL.

CHAPTER I.

INTRODUCTORY.

I INTEND to make an attempt to write the inner biography of Paul the Apostle. I shall try to trace the course of his spiritual history from the day of his conversion to Christianity until the day when he declared himself "ready to be offered." It is a task not of great length, but of great magnitude. It does not need a multitude of pages like the record of his outward biography. It requires no maps nor charts, no study of contemporary men and manners, no consultation of references foreign to his own actual writings. To write a man's inward biography demands before all things the undergoing of a kindred experience and the living of a common life. But if in this respect the task is comparatively easy, it is in another aspect supremely arduous. The difficulty of writing St Paul's inward biography is not the difficulty of statement, but of discovery. The historian of his outward life has the facts already made to his hand, but he who would record the history of his spiritual experience must begin by interpreting the facts. The outward historian has the narrative of the Acts before him, and he has simply, with intelligence and observation, to follow the course of the stream. But the historian of the inner life has before him only a series of letters, written at different times and dictated to different readers; and before he can even enter on his labours, he requires to arrange and to examine the order of those spiritual sentiments whose historical unfolding is to be the subject of his narrative.

There is a preliminary difficulty which meets us at the very door. I have spoken of arranging and examining the order of Paul's spiritual experience. I shall be asked at the outset what right I have to assume the existence of such an order. Was not this man inspired, and does not inspiration imply the denial of any such development? In the case of an ordinary man, it is legitimate to consult his correspondence with a view to determine the gradual unfolding of his mental life. It is legitimate in such cases to refer a certain utterance to a certain period, and to explain a particular view by its congruity with a particular stage of progress. But is such a

process admissible in the case of one who, by supposition, was struck by the light of heaven—who
was lifted by a Divine inspiration from out the
common level on which moved his country and his
age, and translated by a seemingly instantaneous act
into a height of heavenly illumination? That is the
question which meets us on the threshold, and for
the present bars the threshold. It is by reason of
this question that the inward biography of St Paul
has remained to this day one of the most untrodden
fields in history. Volumes have been written on
his outward life, pages have been expended on his
missionary journeys, sermons have been multiplied
on the lessons of his perils and his trials,—but the
history of the man himself, the record of his inward
experience, the study of his spiritual development
from day to day, has as yet occupied little attention. We have a series of letters, professedly written
by his hand, extending in chronological order from
the First Epistle to the Thessalonians to the Second
Epistle to Timothy, but it has rarely occurred to us
to imagine that the chronological order of these
letters marks a mental order too. It has rarely
occurred to us to inquire why the Epistle to the
Thessalonians should have had an earlier date than
the Epistle to the Romans, or why the Epistle to the
Romans should have occupied a previous place to
the letter inscribed to the Ephesians. It has commonly been taken for granted that the teaching in

these respective documents exhibits no other mark
of progress than that of an earlier and a later note
of time.   And the reason of this is not hard to find.
It has been assumed that Paul, being an inspired
man, ought not to be a creature of flesh and blood;
that, being a recipient of the Divine life, he should
be freed from the conditions of human development.
He may write to Thessalonica in the year 52, and
to Timothy in the year 68, but we are not allowed
to believe that these sixteen years covered a growth
of experience.   It is deemed irreverent to suppose
that a man might put his hand upon any of St
Paul's letters and determine its age by the degree of
its maturity.   Such a permission would be the confession of a progress from the imperfect to the perfect, and the admission of such a progress is held to
be incompatible with the claim to be an inspired soul.

The question is—Is it so ?   Is the idea of inspiration incompatible with the idea of progress ?   If we
were dealing with any other religion than Christianity, I would without hesitation answer Yes !   The
peculiarity of all other religions consists, to my mind,
in this—that they regard the inspiration of a human
soul as something which lifts that soul outside of
its humanity, something which raises it beyond the
conditions of progress and places it in an atmosphere from which it can never be moved.   But
the Christian idea of inspiration is distinguished
from the heathen or Gentile idea precisely by the

negation of this belief. Christianity in its very key-note strikes upon a new conception; it declares that the inspiration of a human soul is no longer to be regarded as an abolition of its human growth or a transcending of its human development. The life of the Christian Founder is introduced into the world as a divinely inspired life, but the Divine inspiration is allowed to unfold through the stages of the infant, the child, the youth, and the man. It is represented as a growth in wisdom and in know-ledge and in Divine favour. Each stage is full up to the measure of its capacity, but the capacity is in no case transcended before the time. The childhood is perfect, but it is the perfection of a child—a per-fection which consists in a will subject to authority and a mind inquiring in the temple of truth. The youth is perfect, but it is the perfection of obedi-ence in the path of youth—of consenting to abide in obscurity until the fulness of the time be come, and submitting to support its way by the result of daily toil. The dawn of manhood is perfect, but it is the perfection peculiar to the dawn—the perfection which can stand upon the mount of temptation and choose between the alternatives of right and wrong.

Such is the leading idea of Christian inspiration —the growth of the Divine through the capacities of the human. Appearing at the very outset in the life of the Christian Founder, it is designed to be repeated in the lives of all His followers. For it must not be forgotten that Christianity in its original manifestation is not the reception of a system of doctrines, but the assimilation to a particular type of life. It is the leading thought of the New Testament, and it is the specially prominent thought in the writings of St Paul, that the life of the Christian Founder is repeated in the lives of His followers, that the stages of each Christian's experience are designed to be a reproduction of those stages by which the Son of man passed from Bethlehem to Calvary. Paul has himself declared[1] that the process of Christian development is a process whereby the follower of Christ is " transformed into the same image from glory to glory." No words can more adequately express his view of the nature of this new spiritual order. It is a transformation not only into the image of the Master, but into that progressive form in which the image of the Master unfolded itself. The Christian is to ascend by the steps of the same ladder on which the life of the Son of man climbed to its goal; he is to proceed " from glory to glory." He, too, is to have his childhood, his youth, and his manhood; his period of subjection to outward authority; his time of temptation in the wilderness; his experience of burden-bearing in the haunts of the great city. He is to have his time of growth and his age of maturity, his season of inquiry in the temple of truth, and his day

[1] 2 Cor. iii. 18.

for imparting the fruits of his ripened mind. No man can read Paul's epistles without being impressed on every page with the predominance of this thought. The key-note of his whole teaching is " Christ in you." He tells us that there is a stage in which Christ is only *formed* within the soul—a period which is no more than the process of being born.[1] He tells us that there is a time in which the religious life is, like the beginning of all other life, so much under the dominion of sense that it can only be fed by the sensuous.[2] He tells us that the manifestations of each Christian period must be proportionate to the capacities of that period—that the child must speak as a child, understand as a child, think as a child.[3] He tells us that the goal of Christian manhood, which is the goal of perfect understanding, is only to be reached in that day when the soul shall have completed its stages of rooting and grounding, and shall have attained the stature of universal love.[4]

Is it to be supposed that Paul himself was an exception to this rule ? Is it to be thought for a moment that the man who, of all others, lays such stress on the progressive nature of the Divine life should have been, or should have believed himself to be, exempt from that progress ? We have thirteen letters professedly written by his hand—letters distinguished from most of such public documents by

[1] Gal. iv. 19. [2] 1 Cor. iii. 1, 2.
[3] 1 Cor. xiii. 11. [4] Ephes. iii. 17.

their intense humanness. Seldom have men in their private epistles exhibited such an utter absence of self-consciousness as does the apostle of the Gentiles in these exhortations to the Christian public. He seems to be writing off his guard. He makes us feel that his letters are a revelation of himself—that he is not directing his thoughts, but being borne along by them. We feel that his ideas are too rapid for his pen, and that the machinery of writing is an encumbrance. We seem to be in the presence, not of a scribe, but of a conversationalist, a man who is pouring out his whole soul through the vehicle of words, regardless of sequence and regardless of grammar. We are impressed with the conviction that, if ever the mind of man was revealed to his fellow-man, it has been so revealed in these epistolary documents, —documents whose eloquence is greatest in their want of elegance, and which reach their highest summit of literary art in the very point where they display the perfect exuberance of nature. In these letters we have a diary, a record of personal experience extending probably over sixteen years, and displaying with consummate artlessness the inmost heart of the man. No man can read that diary without being impressed with the fact that one day of the life is essentially different from the other. We are made to feel that, in the experience of St Paul, to-day is not the same as yesterday; that the record of life which emerges in 2d Timothy moves on

an entirely new plane from that record of life which
appears in the First Epistle to the Thessalonians.
The question is, Are we to account for this difference
by natural or by unnatural causes ? Are we to suppose that the man revealed a development of experience by an act of ideal imagination, or are we to
suppose that he revealed it because he had actually
passed through it ? Surely the answer cannot be
for a moment doubtful. Surely we are entitled to
believe that what appears on the page of biography
has resulted from the laws of life, and that the
narrative of the apostle's experience is an evidence
of the apostle's growth.

The problem which lies before us is not merely
one of personal interest. It is not simply worthy
of investigation as a study of individual experience ;
it is interesting as a study of the Church's historical
movement. The inward history of St Paul is an
epitome of the inward history of the Church universal. The life of the Gentile apostle exhibits in
his own experience the successive and progressive
stages through which the development of the Christian commonwealth passed during its first hundred
years. Any man who wishes to study the religious
history of that century can find no better key to the
lock than an intelligent perusal of St Paul's epistles ;
for in these epistles he will find a mirror of those
successive phases of thought through which the life
of the Church was unfolded, from its dawning on

the plains of Galilee till the beginning of its spiritual empire in the city of the seven hills.

The history of the Christian Church during its first hundred years is a tale of three cities—Jerusalem, Antioch, and Rome. Whosoever desires to master the philosophy of that history should keep constantly and carefully in his mind the names of these three cities. They mark at once the phases of Christianity's outward fortunes, and the stages of its inward development. The beginning of the new religion is Jerusalem. Christianity appeared in the world as a consummation and fulfilment of Judaism. The first disciples of the faith never dreamed that they were the founders of a new religion, did not even regard themselves as the inaugurators of a distinct party. They no more meant to separate from the Church of Judea than John Wesley meant to separate from the Church of England. Singularly enough, the earliest name by which they were called was just that of Methodists, or "men of the way." [1] They looked upon themselves not as innovators upon the religion of their fathers, but as those who had been privileged to discover the method in which that religion was to become the faith of the world. Accordingly, it never occurred to them that they ought to do anything to indicate their separateness ; it was their constant aim and study to convey the contrary impression. They instituted no new rites,

[1] Acts ix. 2.

they inaugurated no new ceremonies. They made no effort to congregate themselves in places of worship distinct from the common resorts of their countrymen. They met in the same temple where the Pharisees and the Sadducees were wont to assemble; they observed the same hours of prayer which from time immemorial had been prescribed to the Jewish people.[1] They would have stared with astonishment if they had been called disloyal Churchmen, or even broad Churchmen. They professed to be religious conservatives, propagators of the old, defenders of the ancient *régime*. If they had any quarrel it was with innovators, with those who had grafted a subsequent tradition upon the original faith of their fathers. They desired to go back, and the only liberty they claimed was the right to go back to the beginning. They professed to find the warrant for their special mode of preaching, not in the descent of new spiritual revelations, but in the study of those early oracles which had constituted at once the foundation and the glory of the Church of the Jewish nation.

The second stage of Christianity's ancient history was Antioch.[2] The curtain here rose upon a new scene. It was here that for the first time, according to our earliest historian, the disciples of the Christian faith received the Christian name. Hitherto they had borne only the Jewish name, had been undis-

---

[1] See Acts iii.   [2] Acts xi. 26.

tinguished by the spectator from the creed and
customs of their countrymen. But here, in this
Syrian capital, the differences which the home atmosphere had failed to reveal were brought clearly
into view. It began to break upon the minds of
men, to break upon the minds of the first disciples
themselves, that although Judaism might be regarded
as a germinal Christianity, Christianity was far more
than a developed Judaism. I may climb to the top
of a hill by an old familiar road, and to this extent
I am entitled to say that the hill-top is the goal of
that road. But when I have reached the top of the
hill, I am certain to find that it could have been
reached by many other avenues than the one through
which I approached it—that I have no right to regard this summit of my climbing as the exclusive or
peculiar goal of the old familiar road. Now this
was precisely the discovery to which the Church of
the first Christian century attained in the city of
Antioch. It had reached the top of a hill, had
reached it by an old familiar road which hitherto
it had believed to be the only road. But from the
vantage - ground of the summit it found that this
belief had been a delusion. It found that the height
which had been now attained through the steps of
the old *régime* was susceptible of being discovered
through totally different steps. For the first time
in the history of the movement, the Christian religion presented to its friends and to its contempo-

raries the appearance of a novelty. Its novelty lay
in its very aspect of universality. Hitherto it had
believed itself to be simply the flower of Judaism,
but at Antioch it discovered that it was the flower
of the religious spirit itself. Hitherto it had imagined that men could only approach it through
the gate of the temple, but at Antioch it discovered
that the gate of the temple was only one of a multitude of avenues. Accordingly, for the first time,
Christianity exhibited the appearance of a broken
unity. Its votaries were no longer seen following
one common track. They approached it from all
directions; they came to it by the most opposite
roads. The Jew still sought it by the old familiar
portal, still professed to hold that it lay through the
gate of his own national worship. But the represen-
tatives of Gentile nations claimed each his own gate,
and refused to pass through the ancient avenue.
Antioch was the beginning of religious strife, because it was the beginning of religious freedom: the
first-fruit of private judgment is ever unripe. As
the mother-city of Jerusalem receded, there was no
longer any central tribunal. Each man fell back
upon the authority of his own experience, and the
variety of experience produced a variety of schools.
The river was parted and became four heads—the
same four which appeared simultaneously in the
Church of Corinth,[1] and reappeared persistently in

[1] 1 Cor. i. 12.

the churches of the Greek republics. It was the inevitable result of that moment of transition in which Christianity ceased to be the immediate privilege of a race and passed into the possession of universal man.

By-and-by there came a third stage of the drama; a new mother - city began to rise for the young church upon the ruins of the old. The authority of Jerusalem had been superseded by the anarchy of Antioch; the anarchy of Antioch was in turn to give place to the sovereignty of Rome. Christianity had lost its political fountain-head, but it was to find a political ocean; the river had been parted after leaving its source, but it was to be united again on reaching the sea. That common sea where the divisions of the young church were to be merged in a second unity was the city of Rome. As soon as that city received a Christian church, it became the centre of gravity to all other churches. It did so, not because it was the supposed abode of St Peter, but because it was the actual abode of the emperor. It was the imperial and not the episcopal distinction of Rome that made it the seat of the new authority. Long before her bishop had acquired or even claimed the right to exclusive jurisdiction, the city of the seven hills asserted her desire to be the monitory and reconciling mother.[1]   She aspired to be the

---

[1] See Clement's 1st Epistle to the Corinthians, whose date is certainly not later than 95 A.D.

arbiter between the divisions of the Christian community, and she did not aspire in vain. There was
much in the constitution of Rome which made her
fit to be such an arbiter. Gentile to the very core,
she yet exhibited a greater analogy to Judaism than
can be found even in Semitic races. Nowhere with
such prominence were the features of the East and
West blended together. Rome and Jerusalem, in
some respects the opposite poles of thought, had yet
elements in common which ultimately went far to
unite the old faith with the new. Both were based
in their social structure on the recognition of a moral
code, on a sense of the majesty of law. Both placed
in the foreground of that law the idea of justice, the
rendering of rights by man to man. Both in a sense
were theocratic identifiers of the secular with the
sacred; the Jewish king was the Lord's anointed,
the Roman emperor was the head of a priesthood.
Both aspired to a universal dominion, a dominion
which should radiate from themselves as a centre
and embrace in its circumference all ends of the
earth. What is more remarkable still, both seem to
have entertained one common ideal of the nature of
universal dominion. The conception of a kingdom
of God sketched out by the writer of the Pentateuch
is the idea of a number of relatively independent
states, bound together into unity by the recognition
of a common theocratic centre. Such is precisely
the ideal towards the realisation of which the Roman

empire aspired. She, too, aimed at the establishment of a kingdom, not upon the ruins of other kingdoms, but upon the consent of other kingdoms to recognise herself as their theocratic head. She never sought to press out the life of the nations she subdued; she was willing not only that they should preserve their lives, but that they should preserve their individual varieties. She only desired that these individual varieties should consent to circle round a common sun, and agree to accept their independent life as a gift of grace from herself.

It is not surprising that under these circumstances Rome should have eventually become in a strictly literal sense the New Jerusalem. She actually succeeded in being precisely that form of government which the Jewish commonwealth had aspired to be. If the old Jerusalem had possessed strength equal to her will, she would have anticipated that model of empire which imperial Rome achieved. The old Jerusalem's ideal was, without collusion and without imitation, an adumbration of that which appeared in the empire of the Cæsars. So early as the date of the 122d Psalm, there had floated before the mind of a Hebrew poet the image of a city which was to be the uniting centre of surrounding differences—of a city to which, once a year, the conflicting tribes were to go up, and within whose walls they were to become one family. That was the mode of conquest to which, in its best and purest moments, the Jewish theocracy aspired,—not the subjugation of national peculiarities nor the destruction of tribal differences, but the recognition by different tribes of a common centre in the city of Jerusalem. And that was the mode of conquest to which the Roman empire actually attained. The dream of the old Jerusalem was fulfilled in the New. The city of the seven hills became the central city of the world—the place to which the tribes of the earth went up to claim a common brotherhood. Here, for the first time in history, was realised the thought which had been expressed on the very threshold of Jewish literature —the idea of an empire whose component parts were relatively independent, but which found their union in the recognition of a theocratic head. In imperial Rome, as in ancient Israel, the bond which was designed to join the nations of the world was the acceptance of a central seat of government whose authority was supposed to rest on the immediate will of heaven.

In this brief and necessarily superficial sketch, I have been guilty of no irrelevancy. My sole design has been to show what was that outward history of which the life of St Paul was a mirror. For, indeed, it will be found that the main value of this life, from a historical point of view, consists in the fact that it is an epitome, an abridgment, a microcosm, of the first Christian century. The life of St Paul, like the history of his age, is a tale of three cities—Jeru-

B

salem, Antioch, and Rome. Alike in the narrative
of the Acts, and in the order of his own Epistles, the
course of the apostle exhibits a progress from the
city of the Jews to the city of the Cæsars. His life
embraces that period which reaches from the end of
the beginning to the beginning of the end. He appears upon the scene precisely at that stage where
Christianity has ceased to be a merely individual
movement; he disappears from the scene precisely
at that moment in which Christianity begins to be
the centre of the world. We first meet him on the
streets of Jerusalem, incarnating in his own person
all the leading characteristics of his nation, and
carrrying these instincts along with him even beyond the crisis of Damascus. We next meet him
on the streets of Antioch, and find him parting with
much of his old life, waking into a struggle between
the present and the past, and realising a vivid contrast between this world and the world to come.
Then we see him once more in a third and final
attitude. Even before he has reached the city of
Rome he is touched by the culture of the empire,
and when he enters that city he is dominated by its
culture. There rises before him the image of a new
theocracy, wider and more comprehensive than the
old,—the image of a kingdom of God on earth which
shall realise the gospel figure of the branches and
the tree. He sees in anticipation the various races
of men, without sacrificing their nationality, con-

senting to recognise one common head, and united in the acknowledgment of one paramount and sacred sovereignty. His letters henceforth breathe the Roman atmosphere—the atmosphere of reconcilia- tion. His world ceases to be the opposite of the world to come; grace ceases to be the antithesis of nature; Gentile ceases to be the contrary of Jew. The various forms of humanity are beheld as the members of one vast body, each necessary to the other, none adequate in itself; and the bond of union to the whole is a common life of love which enables them, even amidst their varieties, to say, " we being many are one."

Such is the historical interest of the study now before us. It is not, however, in its historical aspect that I intend mainly to pursue it. I want to look at it chiefly from the side of religious experience, and from the standpoint of Paul's personal life. Accordingly, I shall ask leave to disregard almost altogether the narrative of the Acts, to assume that no documents are before me except those thirteen letters which are professedly written by St Paul, and which contain a direct record of St Paul's ex- perience. In taking this course I am not actuated by any doubt of the substantial credibility of the Acts, but solely and entirely by the desire to reach the most immediate sources from which information on this subject can be obtained. The book of Acts is professedly not an immediate source. However much it may be the work of an eyewitness, it is by its own admission the work of an outsider, of one who records the deeds and words of St Paul as they struck his own eye and ear. But to reach the direct source of a biography, we must hear the man speak himself, must arrive at the secret of his inner life by listening to his own inward communings. In the case of Paul we have in our possession such a record—a record which, if discovered for the first time, would be hailed as simply invaluable. I wish in this study to try to imagine that for the first time we had made such a discovery. I shall try to approach the letters of St Paul as if I had found a new document. I shall make an attempt to come to them with a fresh eye, and, as much as possible, with an unbiassed mind. Above all, I shall study to confine myself to that which is strictly normal, that which lies within the range of Christian experience.

The record of a life's development can only begin at the point where that life has begun. It must take notice of its earliest manifestation, but it has nothing to do with the question how that manifestation arose. The earliest manifestation of man's physical life is perhaps an infant's cry, and he who would record the progressive experiences of such a life will require to take notice of the cry. But within the province of this study he is by no means entitled to inquire what was the origin of that sensation which prompted the cry. That is a

perfectly legitimate question, but it is a question
for the apologist and for the scientist; it is outside
the record of the development itself. So is it with
the study now before us. To trace the spiritual
development of St Paul we are required to go back
to his initial experience, but no further. We are
required to put our hand upon the earliest phase
of difference which distinguishes the life of Paul
the apostle from the life of Saul of Tarsus, but it is
outside our province to ask whence that phase itself
arose. To inquire into the origin of the light which
marked for him the boundary of transition from
the old into the new belongs to the sphere of the
apologist, and of the apologist alone. For us it will
be enough to trace the course of the light after it
has risen, and to mark the stages of its progress from
the dawn to the perfect day.

CHAPTER II.

AUTOBIOGRAPHICAL REMINISCENCES.

I HAVE said that the record of St Paul's spiritual experience embraces directly those sixteen years from the writing of 1st Thessalonians to the writing of 2d Timothy. But indirectly it embraces a great deal more. Did it not embrace more, a great part of Paul's life would be to us an unknown land. By the time we meet with him in the First Epistle to the Thessalonians he is already no longer young. He has had behind him a great history, which has left its marks upon him, and made him what he is. What is that history ? Have we any record that can help to bridge the blank space between the hour in which he first accepted Christ and the hour in which he appears upon the scene as the prominent actor in the development of Christ's religion ? Even if we intended to avail ourselves of the narrative in the Acts, we would find little light upon this question. In that narrative the brilliant beginning of the spiritual life of Paul is followed almost instantaneously by a period of eclipse and silence. The man who on the plains of Damascus is seen illuminated by the fire of heaven disappears immediately from our view, and is lost for a time amid the shadows. We meet with him for the first time at Antioch, but Antioch is clearly not his beginning. There is a period of silence in the background which requires to be accounted for, and which is necessary to explain the present attitude of the man. How is that silence to be broken? Where shall we find the materials for filling up the blank between the day of Damascus and the days of Antioch? It cannot be supposed that Saul of Tarsus emerged in the twinkling of an eye from the attitude of an uncompromising Jew to the position of an unbending Gentile; such a transition would be as contrary to spiritual as it would be to natural evolution. We feel instinctively that, in the Christian development of St Paul, Jerusalem must have a place before Antioch. We feel that, wherever and whenever the desiderated record shall be discovered, it shall be the record of an experience rather Jewish than Gentile, and separated by no very violent convulsion from the experience of his former days. The record which shall break the silence will be one which shall exhibit Paul the apostle at the slightest possible remove from Saul of Tarsus, and shall reveal in the features of the incipient Christian the transmitted lineaments of the developed Jew.

Is such a source of knowledge attainable ? I believe that it is. It cannot, as we have seen, be derived from the narrative of the Acts ; there is here a break in the history. But there is another direction from which information may be sought — those very letters of St Paul which belong to a comparatively late stage of his outward life. It will be found that these letters, emerging as they do from the apostle's days of middle age, have yet in them that autobiographical stamp which is the characteristic of letters in general. Written to serve a particular and a present purpose, they yet from time to time throw back a retrospective light. If they contain flashes premonitory of the future, they equally exhibit gleams illuminative of the past. The apostle almost unconsciously takes us into his confidence, and tells us what has been his previous experience. There are many great writers who are able from beginning to end to preserve a strict impersonality ; one would never know from Shakespeare that he had ever been a child or a boy. But Paul is not one of these. Completely absorbed as he is in the study of that which is impersonal, he is yet unable to conceal that there was a time when he understood and spake as a child. Ever and anon in the very heart of his most abstruse discussions there open glimpses of perspective which cast back a light on his past development. If we can succeed in collecting and combining these, if we can conceive any plausible scheme which would account for their chronological order, we shall arrive at a very probable history of that portion of Paul's life which is at present wrapped in silence. We cannot, indeed, on a matter of this sort, expect to reach demonstrative evidence; we must be content to allow some margin for the play of the historical imagination. But we shall at all events have a working hypothesis which, in the absence of any better guide, may serve as a solution of much that is now obscure.

The first of these autobiographical reminiscences is one which brings Paul before us in an attitude quite unique in apostolic history. Every disciple who embraced Christianity made a transition from an old into a new life; to this extent there is nothing peculiar in the experience of St Paul. But St Paul himself tells us that his adoption of Christianity was distinguished from that of the other apostles by the fact that, in embracing it, he made a transition not merely from the old into the new, but from the persecutor into the partisan,—"For I am the least of the apostles, that am not meet to be called an apostle, because I persecuted the church of God. But by the grace of God I am what I am."[1] Here is a biographical reminiscence of far-reaching value, not so much for its own sake as for the inferences which are to be deduced from it. St Paul declares that he occupied a unique

[1] 1 Cor. xv. 9, 10.

attitude in relation to the other apostles. The question which naturally suggests itself is, Why? Looking back from the standpoint of our present knowledge, we should certainly not have imagined, had we not been told, that there had been any difference between the pre-Christian experience of Paul and the pre-Christian experience of his colleagues. Nor, even after we have been told, is it at first sight very easy to account for the difference. Why should the original attitude of Paul towards Christianity have been more hostile than the original attitude of Peter or John or Thomas? There is nothing in the character of Paul which would lead us to expect that he should have manifested any hostility to the name of Jesus; everything the reverse. It is not too much to say that there is a greater inherent congruity between the character of Paul and the life of Jesus than there is between the life of Jesus and the first historical pictures of the character of John. If there ever was a man who, from a human point of view, might have been expected to sympathise with Jesus of Nazareth, that man was Saul of Tarsus. Unlike almost every other of the original disciples, the beginning of his Christian experience exhibited the promise and potence of a sacrificial life. Here, almost alone in the records of early Christianity, we are brought into contact with a man who does not begin by asking an equivalent for the service on which he is about to enter.

We see him from the very outset consenting to leave all and follow Jesus, without ever once asking the question " What, then, shall we have ? " We are impressed in him with the paramount and dominating presence of that sense of duty which is the perpetual foe of self-interest. It never occurs to him to weigh the consequences of the step he is taking; it never enters into his mind to measure the earthly loss by a possible earthly gain. All he knows is that he has heard a voice calling him, and that he has no choice but to obey. He surrenders himself to privation, pain, poverty, for the sake of love, and in so surrendering himself he manifests the ripest fruit of the sacrificial life which had yet been given to the world. Is it conceivable that such a man should, a few hours before, have been manifesting a personal hostility to the character of one who, considered from a purely human aspect, was so pre-eminently and markedly the counterpart of his own soul ?

I answer, it is not. But I ask, Is there anything in the circumstances of the case which warrants us to conceive such a thing ? Is the history of Saul of Tarsus the history of a man who was converted from antagonism to the character of Jesus ? There is not a particle of evidence that in the mind of Saul there ever existed such an antagonism. The opposition in his mind was not to the character but to the name or claim of Jesus. How much he had learned of the narrative of Christ's earthly life we can never know, but the very fact of the silence on this point is strongly confirmatory of the notion that the narrative of Christ's earthly life was not the ground of his antipathy. His antipathy rested on something which was posthumous, on the claim set up by the disciples to the Messianic dignity of their departed Lord. Why that claim should have been repulsive to him we shall presently see; but meantime I wish to direct attention to the marked contrast which this view of the matter interposes between the experience of the unconverted Paul and the experience of the unconverted Peter, Thomas, and John. When we speak of the comparative antipathy of Saul and the other apostles, do we sufficiently consider their comparative difficulties? Do we sufficiently bear in mind that the starting-point of Saul was quite different from the starting-point of the other apostles? Saul began precisely where they ended; their inner room was only his threshold. The starting-point of Saul was the recognition of Jesus as Messiah; but the recognition of Jesus as Messiah was a comparatively late stage in the progress of the primitive apostles. No man can read dispassionately the Gospel narrative, and not be impressed with the fact that the first approach of Jesus to His disciples was personal and not official. The day is far spent before He asks them the question, "Whom do men say that I am; whom say ye

that I am?" Before He asked that question He
had already called them, charged them, organised
them, set them apart for their mission. His aim
was to attract them, not to His greatness but to
Himself; or rather it was to lead them to a recognition of His greatness through a knowledge of Himself. Accordingly the great question was suppressed,
postponed. Men were called at the outset not to
the recognition of a doctrine, but to the acceptance
of a life. They were not asked to believe something
about Jesus, but to believe in Jesus Himself. The
inquiry, who He was and whence He came, was
designedly kept in abeyance. The disciple was
desired to contemplate nothing but the man, to keep
his eye persistently fixed upon that which was
earthly and human. Step by step, unconsciously
to himself, he was attracted into an atmosphere of
love from which it was impossible for him to escape.
Before he knew it he was already taken captive,
already made to feel that the presence of the Master
was a vital element in his joy. And when at last
the Messianic claim was put forth,—when at last
the crucial question came, "Whom say ye that I
am?" the disciple had been so fortified by his past
draught of love that, in spite of the recognised
difficulties of such a confession, he was able with
confidence to say, "Thou art the Christ, the Son
of the living God."

I say, 'in spite of the recognised difficulties of

such a confession.' For it must be acknowledged that the claim of Jesus to be the Messiah was based upon the very ground which to the popular mind of Judea constituted the refutation of such a claim,— the bearing of the cross. That the Son of man, because He *was* Son of man, should be a special sufferer; that the Messiah, by the very reason of His sinlessness, should be a peculiar subject of sorrow; that He in whom the heavenly Father delighted should, just on the ground of that delight, be exposed to a more than ordinary share of human ills,—was a parodox which the mind of the Jewish nation was quite unable to realise. In the view of that nation the mark of Divine sonship was the exemption from sorrow; the token of heavenly favour was the possession of a path through ways of earthly pleasantness. It had become a settled point in the national consciousness that the good man must be the prosperous man—that the perfect man must be the most prosperous of all. Very startling, therefore, must have sounded the announcement which, according to St Matthew,[1] was made immediately after the proclamation of Jesus as Messiah—" that He must go unto Jerusalem, and suffer many things of the elders and chief priests and scribes, and be killed." That it *was* startling is manifest from the sequel. Peter cries out, "Be it far from Thee, Lord: this shall not be unto Thee,"

[1] Matt. xvi. 21.

and receives in return the withering rebuke, " Get thou behind me, Satan." Shall it be asked why an expression of natural affection should have met with so vigorous a repulse ? The answer is plain. It was not an expression of natural affection ; it was the expression of an intellectual dogma—the dogma that suffering is incompatible with Messiah-ship. What excited the indignation of Jesus was the sight of a rock on which the ship must inevitably have foundered, if the movement had not been counteracted by the anchorage in a previous love, — a love founded on human relations, and fostered by personal companionship. The truth is, Peter had here very nearly reached that degree, and had altogether reached that *ground* of antagonism which was afterwards so signally manifested in the opposition of Saul of Tarsus. If Saul's antipathy was more bitter, we know why. It was because in his case there was no refuge in a previous love. Saul had to struggle with the difficulty of the Messianic claim without any aid from the memory of a past companionship. He had to begin where the other disciples ended, and precisely at that point where the other disciples stumbled. What prevented their stumbling from becoming a fall was the memory of their Christian past; Saul of Tarsus had no such past, and therefore he had no such memory. He was called to take his start from the point of offence, and to walk backward into the

paths of pleasantness. He had to begin with the
cross, and thence retrace his steps toward the human
scenes of Galilee. I cannot but think that there is
an autobiographical reminiscence of this in the words
written at a future day, " I count all things but loss
for the excellency of the knowledge of Christ Jesus." [1]
Why should he put the Christ before the Jesus ?
Manifestly because he knew the Christ before the
Jesus, because he was called to behold Him as the
Messiah ere he was allowed to see Him as the man.
The earliest object presented to his gaze was precisely that object which had repelled the gaze of the
first disciples ; he was required to receive the cruci-
fied Messiah before he was permitted to behold the
Prophet of Nazareth.

Now the question arises, Have we any record preserved of Paul's state of mind at this juncture ?
Have we anywhere throughout his writings an indication given of the difficulty which the Christian
problem presented to his own heart ? I think we
have. I believe there is one passage which, although not professedly autobiographical, has yet all
the force of an autobiographical reminiscence, and
opens up a vista of perspective into the days of his
pre-Christian struggle. The words to which I allude
are the well-known declaration, " I am not ashamed
of the Gospel : for it is the power of God unto salvation to every one that believeth." [2]   The famili-

<hr>

[1] Phil. iii. 8.   [2] Rom. i. 16.

arity of the passage prevents us, I think, from seeing its peculiarity. Why should Paul say, "I am not *ashamed* of the Gospel?" Why should he use a negative instead of a positive? Why should he be content with asserting the mere absence of a sense of disgrace, when he might have been expected to exult in a sense of triumphant glory? Is not the reason clear? Is it not plain that Paul deprecates any feeling of shame concerning Christianity, because he has a distinct remembrance of the time when Christianity did present itself to his mind as a thing to be ashamed of? He remembers that the Gospel of Christ originally came before him in a garb of extreme humility, and in an attitude which excited his contempt as a son of Israel—an attitude which impelled him to say, 'I would be ashamed to belong to such a company.' And if we ask what awakened this sense of contempt, the answer is found in this very passage. When Paul says, "I am not ashamed of the Gospel: because it is power," he means to imply that he was at one time ashamed of it from believing it to be weakness. His objection to recognise Jesus as the Messiah originated in the fact that the cross of Jesus was contrary to the current ideal of greatness.

I have already pointed out the strong analogy that subsisted between the Roman empire and the Jewish theocracy. Paul was a member of both. He was environed by the traditions of his nation, and he

was surrounded by the atmosphere of imperialism.
Both ran directly counter to the recognition of a
regal claim which was based essentially on a power
of infinite stooping.   Alike to the Roman and to the
Jew, the ideal of universal dominion was the pre-
eminence attained by becoming the master of men.
The pre-eminence claimed by Christianity was on
precisely the opposite ground; the Son of man was
to be the servant of all.   The thought came to Paul
not only as a novelty, but as an incongruity.   I
know very well that he could have found it in certain passages of the Old Testament.   In after-years
no one wondered so much as he at his failure to discover an idea lying in the very heart of his own
scriptures; he could only attribute his obtuseness
to the blindness produced by materialism, or what
he calls "the god of this world."[1]   None the less, it
remains true that neither he nor his countrymen
ever did discover it while they remained Jews.   The
prophetic indications of a connection between suffering and glory were foreign to the heart of the nation,
and repugnant to her historical traditions; and to
believe that God would manifest Himself through
sorrow, exposed a man to very much the same reproach which is now experienced by any one who
holds the crude belief in a Divine manifestation
through chairs and tables.   The reproach of early
Christianity was analogous to the reproach of

[1] 2 Cor. iv. 4.

modern spirit-rapping—it was believed to indicate
a weakness on the part of the worshipper. Above
all, the idea of death was held to be incongruous
and incompatible with Divine manifestation. The
Jew resembled the Greek in his horror of death, yet
the difference was equal to the resemblance. The
Greek's horror of death was a physical aversion;
that of the Jew was based upon a moral shame.
The Greek revolted from everything which im-
perilled the pleasures of life, and therefore his
revolt from death was prompted by natural fear.
The Jew, on the other hand, was at no time im-
mersed in the luxuries of life; the whole tenor of
his religion was in favour of abstinence and self-
denial. If he had believed death to be a part of
the originally prescribed course of nature,—in other
words, of the original will of God, he would have
accepted it stoically if not resignedly. But he believed it to be something abnormal, irregular, dis-
connected with the first plan of nature. It was to
him the penalty imposed for a violated law, and as
such he feared it. He saw in it the shadow that
eclipsed the face of God, and therefore the valley of
his own humiliation. The Jew feared death for the
same reason that the Brahman feared life—because
he believed it to be a state of separation from the
Deity, the entrance into a land of shades, illusions,
dreams. He never associated his greatest men with
the thought of death; Enoch escaped it, Elijah

passed it by, Moses had a hidden grave, Samuel
was seen to rise again. To the son of Israel, morality was inseparable from immortality; the sting of
death was sin.

Now we have Paul's own words for the assertion
that he was in a very pronounced sense a scion of his
race. He tells us that in him there was a peculiar
meeting of national associations. " If any other man
thinketh that he hath whereof he might trust in
the flesh, I more: circumcised the eighth day, of
the stock of Israel, of the tribe of Benjamin, an
Hebrew of the Hebrews; as touching the law, a
Pharisee." [1]   Every expression of this autobiographical statement is intended to suggest the idea that
the mind of Paul was imbued with a sense of the
necessary connection between physical power and
Messianic glory. He was of the stock of Israel—
a lineal descendant of the man who, as a token
of conquering strength, was declared to be a prince
with God. He was of the tribe of Benjamin—a
member of that community which had produced the
first Jewish king, the king whose name he himself
bore. He was a Pharisee—a follower of that sect
which measured everything by its external results,
and estimated the rewards of virtue by its triumphs
in the face of the world. Such a man, hedged
round on every side by the traditions of the past,
must on every side have been repelled by the

[1] Phil. iii. 4, 5.

spectacle of the cross of Jesus. He was required
to accept Jesus precisely at that point where his
national characteristics were assailed. He was required to acknowledge as Messiah one whom he
believed to be dead; as a scion of the stock of Israel,
as a member of the tribe of Benjamin, as a follower
of the sect of the Pharisees, he was bound to re-
pudiate such a claim. The one marvel is not his
original opposition, but his subsequent conversion.
The problem is not to account for Saul's virulence
in comparison with the other disciples, but for the
fact that, with such ground for a comparatively
great antagonism, he should ultimately have manifested a faith and love and zeal to which the other
disciples in their ripest moments never attained.

It is true, Paul ultimately came to the conclusion
that the sacrificial life of the Gospel had in it that
very element which had attracted him in Judaism—
the element of power. But the very expression
in which he announces this discovery is significant.
He says "it is the power of God *to every one that
believeth.*" He means to say that the beauty of the
building is quite apparent when a man has once
got inside the house. But this implies that in the
view of Paul there was a discrepancy between the
inside and the outside appearance. The passage, in
fact, has all the force of a biographical note, and
throws back a light upon Paul's original relation to
Christianity. It virtually tells us that he found in

the inside precisely the opposite of what he expected
to find—power instead of weakness. We can readily
understand how such a discovery should have formed
a bond of constancy to Christianity after he had
once embraced it, but the problem still remains
unsolved why he should have embraced it at all.
The secret of Christianity's sacrificial power lay, according to Paul, in the interior of the building.   It
could not, therefore, have been its sacrificial power
which drew Paul from the outside. We want to
know, not what kept him in, but what let him in ;
not what enabled him to remain steadfast to his
discipleship, but what originally made him a disciple.
He now stands before us in the exterior of the
building, and to his eye the edifice looks so repulsive and uninviting that he cannot bear to enter it.
There is a stone before the door which is to him
a rock of offence—the stone which originally lay
on the sepulchre of Jesus. He cannot accept as his
Messiah one who, in the sight of men, has passed
through the ordeal of death, and been laid in an
earthly grave. Who shall roll away the stone from
the door ? Who shall remove the preliminary pre-
judice which to Paul bars the threshold ? Who
shall reconcile to him the claim of Jesus to be the
Messiah with the undoubted and notorious fact that
He "has been evidently set forth crucified"? [1]

Now let us try to dismiss from our minds any

[1] Gal. iii. 1.

thought of documentary evidence. Let us, in the
meantime, ignore the knowledge that we have any
subsequent record of the immediate cause of Paul's
conversion. Let us confine ourselves strictly to the
fact that he has been confronted by these two
seemingly incongruous elements—the claim of Jesus
to Messiahship, and the consciousness that Jesus
had been crucified. The question is, In what direction could a solution of the problem be found
whereby Paul could accept the Messiahship of Jesus
in spite of the fact of His crucifixion? I have no
hesitation in saying that there was only one possible
direction in which such a result could be found. If
Paul accepted Christ at all, he could only do so on
the ground of a belief that, in spite of the crucifixion,
Christ was still alive. In the very nature of the case
Paul was bound to be the apostle of immortality.
Circumstanced as he was, it was not possible for
him to be a Christian in any form except on the
basis that Christ was risen. I am not prepared to
say that the same holds true for the other apostles.
They did not originally come to the Christ but to
the Jesus. Their first approach to the Son of man
was not on the ground of His Messiahship, but on
the ground of His humanity. They were drawn to
Him not by an exhibition of His power, but by a
vision of His gentleness, by a sight of His human
sympathy. Such an impression, independent as it
was of Messianic manifestations, could not have

been affected by the contradiction of these manifestations.   Even though the death of Jesus had
been to the first apostles the closing scene of all,
even though the shadow of the grave had to them
never been eclipsed by the vision of His immortality, there is no improbability in the thought that a
Christian community might have been founded on
the basis of His humanity alone; what the sacrificial
life of Buddha has done, the sacrificial life of Jesus
well might do.   But Paul did not originally approach
Christ as a man.   What he was called to behold
was not a human life, but a Messianic claim, and a
Messianic claim in behalf of one who had been
carried to the grave.   Into the portal of the grave
Paul could not enter to meet with Jesus.   The conception of death was incompatible with the conception of Messiah.   Had he known Jesus as a man,
he would have reverenced Him as a man, and his
reverence would not have been eclipsed even by the
shadow of death.   But he was called to know Him
first and foremost as a Divine manifestation, and
with such a recognition the shadow of death was
at variance.   Before Paul could even approach
Christianity, he required to see that shadow superseded.   To make him a Christian, it was necessary
that, first of all, the thought of death should be
annulled by the vision of immortality, and that
beyond the heights of Calvary there should be discerned the sunlit peaks of Olivet.

All this, I say, might be gathered from the nature of the case, irrespective altogether of documentary evidence. But when we turn to the documentary evidence our expectation is wonderfully confirmed. We leave out of account the narrative of the Acts, yet perhaps nowhere is the narrative of the Acts more strikingly corroborated than in the view that Paul's Christian experience began with the vision of Christ's immortality. When he is speaking to that nation which of all others reverenced most the idea of physical strength, he bases Christ's claim to its recognition on the fact that He had triumphed over death, that He was "declared to be the Son of God with power, by the resurrection from the dead." [1] When he is speaking to the same nation of the ground of his Christian confidence, he again lays the main stress on the vision of Christ's immortality, "who is he that condemneth? It is Christ that died, yea rather, that is risen again, who is even at the right hand of God." [2] But to my mind the passage on this subject which of all others most trenchantly illustrates Paul's position is his remarkable aspiration contained in his letter to the church of Philippi, "that I may know Him, and the power of His resurrection, and the fellow-ship of His sufferings." [3] I have called it a remark-able aspiration, because it seems to invert the natural order. Why did not Paul say, "that I may know

[1] Rom. i. 4.   [2] Rom. viii. 34.   [3] Phil. iii. 10.

Him, and the fellowship of His sufferings, and the power of His resurrection"? Is not this the historical arrangement in which the events of the life of Jesus actually presented themselves? Undoubtedly it is. But it is not the order in which the events of the life of Jesus presented themselves to Paul's experience; that which was last, to him came first. The passage has a biographical ring in it. It tells us that Christ had come to the man of Tarsus in the inverted order of His own life. To the primitive disciples the Christian revelation had presented itself in its natural and historical order— first the Man, then the fellowship with His sufferings, and, last of all, the power of His resurrection. To Paul the Christian revelation presented itself in exactly the opposite arrangement; it began with the crown, and it went back to the cross. Paul's vision rested first of all on that which was supernatural and superhuman, and he had thence to retrace his steps into that which was earthly and historical; he began with the "power of the resurrection," he passed next into "fellowship with the sufferings," and he ended with the recognition of that which identified Christ with humanity. His spiritual life was in one sense a progress from Damascus to Galilee; it had to find its terminus where that of Peter and John had found its beginning. Its goal was to be the discovery of that perfect bond of humanity which bound the heart of the disciple to

the heart of the Master, and in reaching that discovery it attained the completion of its journey
precisely where the first apostles had begun.

We have now arrived at a definite point, and a
very important point — the beginning. We have
reached a spot which we can make the starting-
place of Paul's Christian experience. We have
found that in the nature of the case it was necessary
that Paul should begin with the vision of Christ's
immortality ; his very conception of the Jewish
Messiah made it imperative that, at the outset, he
should see the form of Jesus dissociated from the
trappings of the grave. We have seen that this
expectation is confirmed by documentary evidence,
and precisely by that documentary evidence which
in such a case is of the greatest value—the personal
testimony of Paul himself. Here, then, is a centre
from which we may legitimately take our departure.
Independently altogether of the narrative in the
Acts, and from the simple testimony of St Paul's
own autobiographical recollections, we have been
driven to the conclusion that the beginning of his
Christian experience was a vision of the exalted
Christ. It by no means follows, however, that his
vision of the exalted Christ was reached through
a sense of personal exaltation. The peculiarity of
Paul's experience lies in the fact that he came to
the recognition of Christ's glory by passing through
a phase of individual depression. Whether literally

or metaphorically, we are bound to accept the statement that by him the golden gates were first seen
through dimmed eyes. We have no need to travel
beyond the testimony of his own epistles, nor beyond
those epistles whose testimony is most unquestioned,
in order to recognise the fact that the beginning of
Christian experience was to him the beginning of
struggle. Saul of Tarsus exhibits no struggle; Paul
the apostle on the very threshold meets us as a man
of conflict. From that hour when his eye first rested
on the immortal glory of Christianity, he seems to
have awakened to the perception of his own natural
weakness and nothingness; the period of the exalting revelation was the period of the depressing thorn.
It is from this stage, and not from any pre-Christian
stage, that we must date the opening of that great
spiritual battle which he himself describes as the
war between the spirit and the flesh. The exaltation to the third heavens and the buffeting influence
of the thorn are the respective parents of these two
subsequent tendencies which contended within him
as the inner and the outer man—tendencies which,
when reconciled in one direction, broke out anew in
another, and were only lulled to rest in the mature
ripeness of a peaceful old age. A consideration of
the initial movement of these tendencies in the heart
of Paul will engage our attention in the following
chapter.

CHAPTER III.

AUTOBIOGRAPHICAL REMINISCENCES
(continued).

IN the previous chapter we arrived at the boundary-line between the life of Saul of Tarsus and the life of Paul the apostle. At the opening of the present chapter we shall require to step over that line. I have already said that the record of life's beginning does not lie within the history of development. Shall any man put his hand upon the exact spot which forms the point of transition from one stage into another? I may set up a wall between two countries, two provinces, two fields, and I may say that this wall is the boundary-line between them. Yet, philosophically speaking, which here means strictly speaking, I have not by such a process reached any point of transition. The point of transition lies somewhere within the breadth of the wall; that is all the knowledge which I can profess to have attained. Now, what is true in geography is true also in human history. I cannot put my hand upon the

spot which forms the immediate boundary-line between any two periods of man's existence,—cannot
say, 'here youth ends, and here manhood begins.'
I can go to either edge of the stream, can distinguish
on either side the colour of the soil, can mark on
either bank the size and number of the pebbles, but
the stream itself eludes me; it belongs to a transcendental region which the eye is unable to explore.

One thing is certain,—wherever the point of transition lies between the old life and the new, it lies
not without but within the life. No external circumstances, however striking, would be adequate
in themselves to explain that transition. If we
were writing the outward history of St Paul, we
would be expected to begin with the narrative in
the ninth chapter of Acts. We would be expected
to follow the man of Tarsus in his march from
Jerusalem to Damascus, to mark the sudden arrest
of his journey, to witness the light from heaven
which confronted him, and to tell how, in the
presence of that light, the persecutor fell prostrate
to the earth. But even when we had done all this,
we should not be one step nearer to the discovery
of the real point of transition. The writer of the
Acts himself confesses that he has not put his hand
upon the boundary - line between Saul and Paul.
The words, "it is hard for thee to kick against the
goads," are very suggestive. They carry us back to
something behind the light. They tell us that in

the heart of the man of Tarsus there had been a previous struggle—that the very vehemence of his opposition to Christianity had part of its foundation in a desire to stifle thought. They tell us that the outward light had set fire to already existing material, had kindled into a blaze the accumulated product of years, and had effected its seemingly sudden transformation by its contact with elements that had long and silently been gathering in the soul.

And if we turn to Paul's own testimony, we shall find this view of the subject marvellously confirmed. In one of his letters in later life he thus expresses his consciousness of a boundary - line between the old and the new, " It pleased God who separated me from my mother's womb"—*i.e.,* set me apart from the moment of my birth—"to reveal His Son in me." [1] There are two things to be observed in this passage. The one is, that Paul is not himself prepared to lay his hand upon an ultimate point of transition. It seems indeed to him that in one sense he had always been a Christian. He felt as if God had set him apart even from his birth, had caused him from the very first hour of his being to be surrounded with influences which had made it possible for him at some time to see a light from heaven. The other is, that to the retrospective consciousness of Paul the point of transition from the old into the new was not without but within. " It pleased God

[1] Gal. i. 15, 16.

o reveal His Son in me." Looking to the circum-ances of the light from heaven, we should havexpected him to have said "*to me.*" We shouldave expected that Paul would have attributed tohe outward catastrophe that change in his naturehich at all events it accelerated and manifested.ut Paul knew better. He knew that a revelationrom without is a contradiction in terms—that noxternal manifestation, however striking, could pos-ibly reveal God to the soul. He insists upon thisact constantly, pertinaciously, at times even polemi-ally. He says elsewhere, " God, who commandedhe light to shine out of darkness, hath shined *in**our hearts,* to give the light of the knowledge of thelory of God in the face of Jesus Christ." [1]   Heeclares, in language more pronounced still, " Eyeath not seen, nor ear heard, neither have enterednto the heart of man, the things which God hathrepared for them that love Him. But God hathevealed them unto us by His Spirit." [2]   No wordsould express in stronger terms Paul's repudiationf the thought that any mere material mechanismould be the source of Divine revelation. He doesot mean, as is popularly thought, that the sightsnd sounds of heaven are grander than the sightsnd sounds of earth, but rather that in its deepestssence heaven is not sight and sound,—that noutward light, even though above the brightness of

---

[1] 2 Cor. iv. 6.   [2] 1 Cor. ii. 9, 10.

the sun, could for a moment illuminate a human spirit, unless that spirit had elsewhere been illuminated by an inward glow.

But we must now advance a step further. However inward the beginning of the new life be, however subtle in its working, however inscrutable in its immediate point of transition, there is yet a definite moment in which its possession begins to be realised. The sun has actually risen before the eye perceives its rising, but the eye can detect the time when it does perceive its rising. So is it in the spiritual world. No man can point to the precise moment of transition between the old life and the new, but every man may photograph the moment when the new life was first realised by him as a part of his being. Now, in the spiritual experience of Paul there was clearly such a moment of realisation. He is himself quite conscious that he is standing on an opposite bank of the stream to that which he occupied yesterday; yesterday he was a persecutor, to-day he is a friend. What has led him to this realisation? It is a question perfectly legitimate and purely scientific. The origin of a change is one thing, the realising of a change is another and a very different thing. There must have been a time when Paul became conscious in himself of an altered attitude towards Christianity—a time from which it became impossible for him to be a persecutor any more. Have we any clue to the circumstances in

D

which this experience was realised? Have we any indication, from the writings of Paul himself, of the nature of that influence which first led him to recognise the fact that he had, from the hour of birth, been dedicated to Christ?

I think we have. One thing is quite clear, that to the mind of Paul the first conscious transition did not present itself as a voluntary one. In speaking of that transition, he says, "by the grace of God, I am what I am." [1] Now, let it be remembered that in the New Testament the word "grace" has always a definite meaning. It always implies something opposed to the natural will. It is the opposite of "glory." It is the direct antithesis of our English word "grace," which means a naturalised beauty, a symmetry which has become indigenous to the life. Scriptural grace, on the other hand, implies the revelation of something which is not natural to the life, not symmetrical with its proportions, not consonant with its aims. It is the beginning of struggle, the presentation of a point of resistance, the first sense of an impersonal obstacle which has put itself in the way of the development of my own will. When Paul refers his moment of realisation to an act of grace, he really means to refer it to the encountering of an antagonistic experience.

In another passage he himself gives very clear expression to this view. He says, " lest I should be

[1] 1 Cor. xv. 10.

exalted above measure through the abundance of
the revelations, there was given to me a thorn in
the flesh, the messenger of Satan to buffet me." [1]
The act of grace which arrested him on his road to
persecution is here more strictly defined; it is said
to have consisted in the impartation of a thorn to
the flesh. It is the same thought to which he has
already given utterance in speaking of the inward
light which has illumined his heart, "we have this
treasure in earthen vessels, that the excellency of
the power may be of God, and not of us." [2] He
means to say that the recognition of Christianity's
truth could to him be no subject of personal boast-
ing. He had not arrived at that knowledge by an
act of his own will; he had been driven into it. It
had come to him through an arrest of his own will,
through an impediment which had been thrown
across his path, through the encountering of a hostile force which had struck him to the ground. His
illumination had entered through the gate of his
humiliation; his treasure had been conveyed to him
in earthen vessels; his heavenly vision had been
communicated through the medium of an earthly
thorn.

What, then, was this thorn? It has been a subject of much dispute amongst commentators. Was
it of the nature of a physical calamity, or did it bear
the character of a moral stain? Each of these views

[1] 2 Cor. xii. 7.   [2] 2 Cor. iv. 7.

has been advocated on grounds which I think irrele-
vant. On the one hand, it is urged that when Paul
designates his calamity "a thorn in the flesh," he
clearly points to some physical privation; but every
student knows that in the vocabulary of St Paul the
fleshly is by no means necessarily synonymous with
the material. On the other hand, it has been urged
that, when Paul styles his thorn "a messenger of
Satan," he cannot be speaking of a merely physical
calamity. If Paul had been an Englishman, such an
argument would have been unanswerable. But Paul
was a Jew, and, being a Jew, he used the language
of his nation. In the language of that nation all the
sorrows of life were the messengers of Satan. No
matter from what source they came, whether from
without or from within, whether from the body or
from the soul, they were regarded by the pious
Israelite as the enemies of his peace and the penalties of his sin. To the mind of a son of Israel the
loss of sight was as much the buffeting of Satan as
the loss of temper. "Who sinned, this man or his
parents?" was the question which spontaneously
arose in the view of every physical calamity. There
were spirits which struggled to rise above it; there
were minds which, like the patriarch of Uz, had
glimpses of a higher and holier destination of human
sorrow; but the very strength of their opposition
proved the tenacity of the national belief. The tenacity of that belief was broken by Christianity alone.

Only in the religion of Christ could even such a one as Paul recognise the glory of a cross; to the initial stage of his Christian experience the calamity of his life still remained "a messenger of Satan to buffet" him.

We are not entitled, then, to draw any argument from either expression. The "thorn in the flesh" does not necessarily imply materialism ; the "messenger of Satan" does not necessarily imply the presence of a moral stain. There is, however, one argument which, so far as I know, has not been hitherto advanced, and which seems to me to bear conclusively on the decision of this question. In the sequel of that passage in which Paul speaks of his thorn, he makes his calamity a subject of prayer, "for this thing I besought the Lord thrice, that it might depart from me. And He said unto me, My grace is sufficient for thee; for my strength is made perfect in weakness."[1] I shall hereafter return to these words in another connection; they belong to a later stage in Paul's spiritual biography, and I only notice them now in their bearing upon the nature of that calamity which marked his conscious transition into the kingdom of Christ. Looking at them, however, in this light, it seems to me that they decide the question as to whether the nature of that calamity was moral or physical. Is it conceivable that any man, struggling with a moral defect, and

[1] 2 Cor. xii. 8, 9.

earnestly praying for the removal of that defect, should have either received, or imagined that he received, a denial of that prayer? Is it conceivable that one under the influence of a heated temper, or a jealous disposition, or a lustful passion, should have thought for a moment that the preventive or restraining grace of God would be equivalent to the removal of such a tendency, or that the strength of God could find its perfect manifestation in the effort to struggle with such a weakness? The truth is, in any such case as this, the grace of God is not sufficient for us, does not profess nor desire to be sufficient for us. The climax of the moral life is not grace, but glory; not the struggle with a new atmosphere, but the assimilation of the nature to that atmosphere. The strength of God in the moral world is perfected, not by its restraining influence, but by the removal of all necessity to exert such an influence. It is perfected in that hour in which my will has ceased to choose, in which the element of temptation is no longer present to my heart, and in which the power that used to be restraining has become the impulse of my life.

We must arrive, then, at the conclusion that the thorn in the flesh was a thorn OF the flesh,—that the calamity against which Paul prayed was a calamity of the physical life. If we go on to ask more specifically what *was* that calamity, we can no longer speak so determinately. Throughout his epistolary

writings, Paul has nowhere given us any direct indication of the precise seat of the malady. One
naturally wonders why he should have been so
enigmatical. In a man writing familiar letters to
his familiar friends, we should have expected that,
instead of speaking mysteriously of a thorn in the
flesh, he would have told them that he had become
subject to some particular form of disease. And yet,
to my mind, the reason of his seeming obscurity is
not far to seek. At the time when he wrote these
words, he had not only ceased to grieve over his
thorn, but had come positively to triumph in it. He
did not want his fellow-men to think that his had
been a special case. He wanted them to feel that
they might triumph over their calamities in the
same manner as he had conquered his. To accomplish this end, he thought it best that no suffering
man should be able to say, when referred to him
as an example, 'Paul had quite a different trial
from me.' He thought it best that his own particular trial should not be revealed by name, so that
each suffering man might have a chance of believing
that the apostle's thorn had been his own. He
valued the concealment of his thorn for the same
reason that his countrymen had valued the concealment of the body of Moses—lest men should come
to attach a special and peculiar reverence to that
which was only one of a multitude, and only a single
specimen of a mighty whole.

But while Paul makes no direct reference to the nature of his thorn, I agree with those who hold that he has indirectly, and, as it were, unwittingly, revealed its nature. I agree with those who hold that the preponderance of argument lies on the side of Paul's malady having been an affection of the eyes. The facts, when marshalled together, amount to a moral evidence. He employs an amanuensis —a luxury which would not have been voluntarily appropriated by one in his indigent circumstances. The only part of his letters written by his own hand is the salutation at the end,[1] and the words of that salutation are inscribed in large characters.[2] The largeness of the characters might have had its ground in the desire to emphasise the epistle's genuineness; but there is a very significant circumstance which, to my mind, shakes that view. Almost immediately after directing the Galatians to the large letters he has written with his own hand, Paul breaks forth into the declaration, "I bear in my body the marks of the Lord Jesus."[3] He means to say, "I have no need to get circumcised with a view to have a wound in the flesh; I have already received a wound in the flesh from another and a higher source than any earthly hand." One feels it difficult to avoid connecting such a statement with the immediately foregoing direction to the largeness of his handwriting. And the impression

[1] 2 Thess. iii. 17.   [2] Gal. vi. 11.   [3] Gal. vi. 17.

is wonderfully confirmed when, only a few para-
graphs earlier, we hear him bursting forth into a
strain of tender reminiscence, and reminding this
very church of the sensitiveness, the delicacy, and
the helpfulness which had marked their recognition
of his physical trial, " my temptation which was in
my flesh ye despised not, nor rejected; but received
me as an angel of God, even as Christ Jesus. For
I bear you record, that, if it had been possible, ye
would have plucked out your own eyes, and have
given them to me." [1]

Now, take these passages together and read them
in connection with another passage, which I do not
think has hitherto been seen in this light, " the god
of this world hath blinded the minds of them which
believe not, lest the light of the glorious gospel of
Christ, who is the image of God, should shine unto
them." [2] If we have attached no weight to the
argument of the previous passages, we shall rightly
see no significance in this. But if these passages
have impressed us already with the conviction that
the thorn in Paul's flesh was connected with an
ocular weakness, I think it will be impossible to
avoid the recognition of a fresh allusion here. To
myself it seems evident that Paul, in this latest
passage, is simply making a metaphor of the fact of
his own experience,—is transferring into the life of
the world at large the analogy of that physical crisis

[1] Gal. iv. 14, 15.　　　　　　[2] 2 Cor. iv. 4.

which had marked his transition into the kingdom of God.   For what is it that Paul means to affirm when he says that the god of this world is blinding the natural man to the light of another world ?   Is it not simply this, that in the sphere of spiritual life a man must be made blind in order to see ?   The " god of this world " means the " light of this world." The expression has become obsolete, but it was quite well understood by the men of Paul's day.   There was in that day an incipient belief, which was ere long to become a rampant belief, that the forms of material nature were the work of an inferior deity. Paul does not accept it, but he allegorises it, points out a spiritual sense in which it may be held true. He personifies the spirit of materialism, and calls it the god of this world.   He says that to the natural man those things called the objects of sight are really the objects which prevent sight.   The light and forms of nature are revealers of the present world, but they are the curtains of another world.   They are the shadows which intervene between the eye and a higher and holier light; they intercept and eclipse the rays of a better sun.   Before that better sun can be made visible, the intercepting medium must be destroyed.   The eye must be blinded to the natural light if it would see " the image of God." There must be an eclipse of that which eclipses, a blotting out of that which blots out the view. This world stands in the way of the vision of a higher world; therefore before all things this world must be crucified.

Such is Paul's thought. I submit, however, that it is not a natural thought. It is not an idea which would naturally have occurred to one in Paul's circumstances. Through the writings of the apostle we have become familiar with the doctrine that the outer world must be crucified to the natural man before he can get a glimpse of the spiritual world. But to the mind of a Jew such a doctrine was the wildest of paradoxes. So far from being self-evident, it was to him the reverse of the truth. The preliminary condition of a higher life was to the Jew not the crucifixion but the expansion of the present world. Instead of believing that a man must have outer forms blotted out in order to see the kingdom of God, it was his distinct doctrine that the kingdom of God could only be seen through the extension and the perfecting of outer forms. The man who had his world crucified was essentially the bad man. He was thereby placed in a condition of spiritual blindness, disqualified for beholding God, and debarred from the vision of Divine realities. The Jew could never regard the revelation of the Sun of righteousness as something which was to be purchased by the obliteration of the sun of nature.

Paul's thought, then, was not natural to a Jew. What made it natural to Paul, being a Jew? It seems to me that it was suggested to his mind purely by the fact of a personal reminiscence. It was not a simile derived from the theology of his nation; it was directly opposed to that theology. But it was in harmony with a memory of Paul's own life, and it was that which made it to him the most natural simile in the world. He simply transferred to mankind in general that hour of crisis through which he had passed in his own soul. He remembered a time when he himself had been amply satisfied with the things which are seen and temporal. He remembered a time when the beauty of Christ's religion was completely eclipsed by these things. So insensible had he been to that beauty, that he regarded Christianity as an obstruction to the world's real life. He had resolved to put it down with a high hand; he had set forth against it on a course of persecution. Midway he had been arrested, arrested by the greatest of physical calamities. That world which he believed to be the real world had become unreal,—it had been extinguished for him in black darkness. The proximate cause of the calamity is nowhere revealed; to him there was but one cause. If Paul had known to a certainty that the immediate agent in producing his misfortune had been lightning, or sunstroke, or epilepsy, it would have made no difference on his diagnosis; he would still have referred it to one agency, and to one alone. It had come to him as the arresting grace of God, as a Divine hand interposed between himself and his contemplated victim. On the black canvas which had covered the images of the natural day there arose another image—the form of Him who had been the object of his aversion. It filled the vacant space—not yet indeed as an object of love, but as an object of power; Paul said as Julian afterwards said, "O Galilean, thou hast conquered." Christ was not dead; He was immortal and immortalising. He had proved Himself to be alive by an act of arrestive grace; He had revealed the power of His presence by suppressing all other presences from the apostle's sight. Doubtless it was this sense of revelation by desolation that prompted Paul to see in his own experience an analogy to the creative work of Genesis, and to say that, in giving to him the knowledge of His glory, God had "commanded the light to shine out of *darkness*."

And is it any other thought which is expressed in these other words of Paul, " our light affliction, which is but for a moment, worketh for us a far more exceeding and eternal weight of glory, when we look not to the things which are seen, but to the things which are not seen: for the things which are seen are temporal; but the things which are not seen are eternal." [1] Paul is speaking of two worlds — the world without and the world within. He says that to any man whose gaze is riveted with admiration on the seen and temporal, such a calamity as over-

[1] 2 Cor. iv. 17, 18.

took him must have been indeed appalling. But to
one who has recognised that there is a world behind
the visible world,—to one who has arrived at the conviction that there is a spiritual glory which, to the
natural heart, is eclipsed by the material form, the
vision of his calamity cannot appear as an uncom-
pensated evil. It had in reality worked out for him
a glory far greater than that which it took away,
had revealed a brighter sunshine than the light
which it had put out. It had extinguished the
seen and temporal, but in the very act of doing so,
it had broken down a wall. The veil of the temple
had been rent in twain from the top to the bottom,
and through the aperture had appeared the images
of a higher life.

We are not, of course, bound to assume that the
calamity which overtook Paul remained permanently
in its acute stage. The testimony of his epistles,
with their record of laborious work and incessant
outward struggle, would suggest an opposite inference. I have spoken of Paul as having passed
through an hour of physical crisis, in which he
experienced a total eclipse of the outward visible
world; I have been led to take this view by the
very strong simile he used.[1] But if we regard this
hour of crisis as having amounted to a total eclipse,
we shall require to adopt the view of the later historian that there came a partial recovery. The

[1] 2 Cor. iv. 3, 4.

tenor of Paul's epistles is compatible with a man
who has a thorn, and is consistent with the notion
that his thorn was defective vision, but it is irrecon-
cilable with the belief that he was entirely deprived
of sight. The truth is, as we piece together from
purely internal sources the features of this picture,
as we strive by a combination of the man's own
scattered reminiscences to reconstruct his figure into
its probable height and proportions, we are more
and more impressed with the likeness which that
figure presents to the Paul of historical tradition.
We have woven together colours derived from no
professed history, but simply from the incidental
notices which he gives of himself; and yet, as the
result of the whole, we must confess that hitherto
the Paul of the Epistles has been identical with the
Paul of the Acts. We see the man of the Pharisees
animated by an antagonism to the dead Christ, simply
on the ground that He *was* dead, incapable of being
made a follower except by the belief that death had
to Him been annulled. We see the movement towards persecution arrested midway by what Paul
himself terms an act of restraining grace. We see
the images of external nature extinguished for him
in a stroke of blindness, and on the black canvas
left by his privation we see the imprinting of another
image, destined to surpass for him the brightness of
the sun. We have only to add the supposition that
the full weight of the calamity was subsequently

lightened, and we shall have reached, by an independent process, a portrait which, in all its essential
features, is identical with the old familiar figure of
historical tradition.

We have now come to a point in which the his-
toric tradition must for a time desert us. We are
approaching that period of Paul's life in which the
record of the Acts becomes almost a total blank, and
in which we can have nothing outside of Paul's own
reminiscences with which to compare our picture.
We cannot regard this as a disadvantage, because we
have all along professed to reconstruct the picture
from purely internal sources. Nevertheless, the
very fact that we have here lost sight of historical
tradition has made the region on which we are entering an almost untrodden field. It is a field which
we cannot tread with dogmatic footsteps, nor appropriate with confident claims; we must be content to
walk warily, and to speak with reticence. The mine
from which we gather is still the same. It is a col-
lection of biographical reminiscences scattered up
and down throughout the epistles, yet revealing their
richest vein in the letter to the Galatians — reminiscences often incidental, sometimes rather implied
than expressed, but always opening up glimpses of
perspective, and not seldom suggesting more than
they declare. A consideration of this new field of
study will engage us in the following chapter.

CHAPTER IV.

ARABIA: AUTOBIOGRAPHICAL REMINISCENCES
(*concluded*).

PAUL has now arrived at what may be called a state
of double consciousness. He has for the first time
come into the possession of two natures, and from
this time forth the sense of these two natures is continually present to him.[1] His entrance into Christianity was, by his own admission, an entrance into
internecine war. His experience as Saul of Tarsus
had been an experience remote from struggle; his
struggle began with the first presentation of Christianity. I have already said that in the moment of
his revelation he was exposed to two opposite influences—an influence which exalted, and an influence which depressed. On the one hand, his first
vision of Christ was the vision not of one who was
crucified, but of one who, in spite of crucifixion, was
alive. His earliest meeting with Christianity was
a meeting not with its cross but with its crown.

[1] Cf. Rom. vii. 9 and sequel.

E

Unlike the first disciples, he began at the top of the
hill and was called thence to descend into the
valleys.   On the other hand, his very sense of
Christ's living power was awakened by a personal
humiliation.   It came to him by an arrestment of
his own will—an arrestment which prostrated him,
humbled him, blinded him.   The avenue by which
he reached the conviction of Christianity's glory
was an avenue of individual pain; its central figure
was not a flower but a thorn.   Here, then, at one
and the same moment there were two opposite im-
pulses in the mind of Paul,—the one enlarging, the
other depressing; the one opening up boundless pros-
pects, the other rendering the man cribbed, cabined,
and confined.   Each of these influences must be
carefully weighed.   We have arrived at a period
of Paul's life in which the two tendencies were so
equally balanced that the man was brought for a
few years into a position of equilibrium, in which
the motive on either side was so strong that he was
unable to decide in what direction he should turn,
and was compelled for a space to lie inactive and
unoccupied.   Let us proceed to consider separately
the opposite effects of these conflicting movements.

And let us begin with the effect of Paul's revelation.   I have said that it came to him with the
inspiration of a sense of boundlessness.   He himself
always connects the moment of his conversion to
Christianity with the conviction of his having re-

ceived a call to labour in a missionary field of un-
precedented dimensions. In the passage from Galatians i. 16, already quoted, he says, "it pleased God
to reveal His Son in me, that I might preach Him
among the Gentiles." [1] In these words he asserts in
the most explicit terms, that his call to be a Christian was, at the same time, his call to be a missionary
on a new and a very gigantic scale. No previous
apostle, no previous disciple of the Master, had ever,
in the initial hour of his discipleship, been privileged
to see such a wide field before him. All the predecessors of Paul had believed themselves to be
missionaries, but to all of them it was a matter of
course that they should begin at Jerusalem. The
man of Tarsus alone, the latest comer of all the
band, and the disciple who, at his coming, had seen
least of the personal life of the Master, had a view
of the religious scope and destiny to which the first
Christians were strangers. And can any one fail to
perceive the reason of the difference? Is it not
manifest that Paul's advantage in this matter came
from the very circumstance which was otherwise a
disadvantage—the fact that he had not known the
personal Christ? It was a great privation to him
that he had not lived in the earthly presence of the
Master, had not come into contact with the outward
and local life of Jesus. Yet it was precisely through
this privation that he was enabled to assign to Jesus

[1] Cf. Ephes. iii. 8.

a wider field of missionary enterprise in the work of the immediate present. Christ had first been revealed to him, not as the man of Galilee, but as the spirit of Olivet. His earliest vision of the Master had been the vision of one circumscribed by no time nor space. To the early disciples the Christ had been born at Bethlehem; to the soul of Paul He was born at Damascus. His sense of His living presence was, from the very outset, the sense of a universal presence. It was associated with no land, it was linked with no atmosphere, it was bound up with no environment. We have Paul's own words for the assertion that the impression created by the belief in Christ's resurrection was the vision of one who had risen far above all principalities and powers, and beyond every name which denotes simply a local designation.[1] And as the impression of the risen Christ was the earliest sense Paul had of His presence, we can readily see why to him the hour of revelation was the hour of a missionary call. In the very sight of One whose theatre was the universe, and whose empire was unlimited by earthly boundaries, the apostle recognised the obligation to go and teach all nations. In the very sense that he was in the presence of a Being who had risen above local distinctions, there came to his mind the conviction that in the field of missionary labour local distinctions must lose their power.

[1] Ephes. i. 20, 21.

I shall hereafter show that in the mind of Paul this sense of a universal missionary obligation by no means presented itself as a revolt from the Old Testament; that, on the contrary, his original ideal of a Christian missionary was based purely upon a Hebrew type of thought. In the meantime, however, I wish to direct attention to the fact that, from the very outset of his Christian experience, he was impressed with the greatness of his privilege in comparison with his predecessors and contemporaries. There is a very striking passage which seems to me to express, in the most direct terms, Paul's conviction of having a unique and original position. Speaking of the appearances of the risen Christ, he says, "last of all He was seen of me also, as of one born out of due time."[1] What is the meaning of the expression, "one born out of due time"? There are two possible ways in which a man may be born out of due time; he may come into the world too soon, or he may come into the world too late. Which is Paul's case? So far as I know, the universal interpretation has been hitherto in favour of the latter view. Paul is popularly supposed to be uttering a complaint that he had not been privileged to behold the earliest dawn,—that his had not been the joy of looking upon the earthly face of the Master; he had been born too late for that. And yet, is it not

[1] 1 Cor. xv. 8.

evident, from Paul's own writings, that he himself
would have repudiated such an interpretation? He
would have denied the truth of the statement on
which it is based. He is never weary of insisting
on the perfect equality of privilege between his
vision of the risen Christ and that vision of the
Christ which the first disciples beheld. It is precisely on this ground that he claims an equal
apostleship, and asserts his right to exert the same
authority. Moreover, if the Greek word be pressed
out to its legitimate meaning, it will bear no other
sense than that of "one born too soon." The figure
is that of a premature birth. It seeks to describe
one who has come into the world at a stage earlier
than his legitimate time. The truth is, so far is
Paul from looking upon himself as behind the age,
that he is impressed, beyond all things, with that
sense of solitude which comes from being advanced
beyond one's day. He feels himself to be an
anachronism, not on the ground of being in the
rear, but on the ground of being in the van. His
first vision of the Master has been an altogether
different vision from that which greeted the eyes
of his contemporaries. He has seen the Christ,
not as a local personality, not as a historical man
environed by a particular age and circumscribed by
a special soil, but as a life risen above all principalities and powers and transcending all temporal
conditions. And the effect of that vision has been

to widen his own view of the missionary field; it
has been to him equivalent to a Gentile call. Can
we fail to see how such a perception must have been
to Paul, itself, a sense of solitude? He felt that he
had been privileged to see what others had not seen,
what others even yet did not believe. The final
apparition of the Son of man had placed him outside the gates of Judaism—not indeed as yet very
far beyond them, as we shall hereafter see, nevertheless clearly and distinctively on the other side. He
felt that he was standing in advance of his fellows,
on a plain which hitherto had been unfrequented,
and where he found himself alone. He had been
called to a solitary privilege—the privilege of recognising the fact that the Gentile was equal to the
Jew; and he expressed at once the dignity and the
loneliness of the position by declaring that Christ
had been revealed to him as to "one born out of due
time."

Why, then, does not Paul rush instantaneously to
the fulfilment of his mission? He has received a
revelation that Christianity is a religion for man as
man; why does he not hasten to proclaim his discovery? He has recognised the truth that the
Gentile has an equal right with the Jew; why
does he not forthwith become the apostle of the
Gentile? That he does not do so is transparent on
the very surface of the narrative. The very obscurity that hangs over this part of his life is a proof

that during this period his life had undergone a temporary relapse. Instead of the moment of Christian conviction being followed instantaneously by a career of Christian action, we are confronted by a spectacle which appears, at first sight, like a falling asleep again. The man introduced to our notice as a percipient of Christ's exaltation is almost immediately afterwards utterly withdrawn from view. We see him on the Jewish bank of the river as a defender of the old world; we see him on the Christian bank as a promised defender of the new; but almost the next instant he disappears from both banks. We seek him and he is not found, or at least is only found as the result of his own confession. If Paul had not himself told us where he was during this interval, we never should have gathered it from history. The man has in the meantime degenerated into a cipher, and the course which promised to be a triumphal march has been arrested by an hour of lethargy. How are we to explain this anomaly of human nature?

The reason in plain language is simply this, Paul was not ready for his destiny. He recognised it clearly, at least he recognised what it ought to be, but he experienced the same sense of diffidence which had characterised the call of his ancestor Moses. For this brings us to consider the second of those influences which at this period acted on the apostle's mind. We have seen that his first vision of the Messiah was the vision of an exalted Christ, and that to this extent the moment of his conscious conversion was a moment of spiritual elevation. But from another side it was also a moment of depression; the vision had come to him through an outward cloud,—the light had shone " out of darkness." He had purchased his recognition of Christ by the experience of a physical thorn—a thorn which had come to him as a process of crucifixion. But Paul himself declares that there are two kinds or degrees of crucifixion; the world may be crucified to me, or, I may be crucified to the world. He says, in a passage which I think certainly autobiographical,[1] that he himself has passed in succession through each of these. He did not all at once reach the stage of being crucified to the world,—of having his heart resigned to the calamity which had befallen him. His original experience was simply that of having the world crucified to him, of being conscious of a sense of loss and deprivation. There was a time, he tells us, in which his attitude under the chastening hand of God was merely a passive attitude; he bowed beneath it, but he did not acquiesce in it. It brought to him a feeling of numbness, a sense of utter prostration. The old man within him was dead, but the new man was not yet alive; Egypt had been torn from his sight, but Canaan had not yet appeared. His was no abnor-

[1] Gal. vi. 14.

mal experience ; there is not a spiritual mind which
has not passed through it.   There is all the difference in the world between a passive and an active
resignation, between a mind that is dumb and unmurmuring, and a mind that is acquiescent and
alive.   It is one thing to accept a thorn as something which comes from a mysterious and incom-
prehensible Will ; it is another thing to accept it,
and to wear it as a flower.   The former state is the
condition in which the world is crucified to us; the
latter is the condition in which we are crucified to
the world.   Paul was as yet only in the first state.
He had received his calamity, and he was dumb
before its presence, but he had not yet accepted
his calamity as a possible road to glory.   That stage
awaited him in the future, but the time was not yet ;
he was for the present simply in the position of one
who is astounded and paralysed.

Does it seem strange to us that a man like Paul
should have been in this position ?   Does it seem
unworthy of his moral greatness, that even for a
moment he should have bent beneath the weight
of a physical thorn ?   It would undoubtedly have
been so if Paul had been a Gentile.   But Paul was
a Jew, and he was none the less a Jew because he
had become a Christian.   To the mind of a Jew
physical calamity was inseparable from moral delin-
quency.   What Paul said, at an after date, of death,
he would have said now of his physical thorn : its

sting to him was sin. I do not indeed believe that at this period his conscience had awakened to the full sense of the struggle between the old life and the new; it is only through the ripeness of the new life that the barrenness of the old can be discerned. But although the conscience of the *man* was as yet comparatively dormant, the conscience of the *missionary* was already on fire. Let us remember what it was to be a missionary, or, as men then called it, an apostle. It was to join the order of a new priesthood. Now it was of the very essence of the Jewish religion that a priesthood should be physically unblemished; any defect in the corporeal frame was an immediate disqualification for such a ministry. It was no admiration of Greek symmetry which led the son of Israel to such a conclusion: Greek symmetry was the furthest thing in the world from his sympathy and from his heart. His abhorrence of corporeal blemish came from his abhorrence of mental defect. It was because to him the body and the soul were one man that in any blemish of the body he beheld a blemish of the moral nature. He desired that the priests and ministers of his religion should be free from outward stain, simply and entirely from his conviction that the presence of an outward stain implied the presence of an inward deformity; and he valued the spotlessness of matter because he believed it to be an index of the spotlessness of mind.

Now Paul had no doubt in his own heart that his physical thorn was the result of a moral deformity. However much in after-years he recognised it as a grace, it had come to him in the meantime as a barrier to the progress of his life. It had presented itself to him as an arrest of his own will,—a prohibitory fence which said, "hitherto shalt thou go, and no further." It had marked him out as an object of Divine reprobation; it had revealed him to the world as one who bore in his own body the sign of God's displeasure. Under these circumstances, what right had he to be a missionary? There had come to him, through his intellectual nature, a wider and grander view of the immediate destiny of Christianity than had ever been possessed by the eye of mortal man; but was it to him anything more than that vision from the top of Nebo which his ancestor had been permitted to see, but in whose realisation he was not allowed to share? There had been revealed to him a new gospel, or rather that hidden wisdom which had slept eternally in the old; but how could he, with a blemished, tarnished name, presume to be the prophet of this evangel? Did he not carry in his own person the credentials of failure? did he not bear in his physical weakness the proof that his mission was not real?

And so Paul, like Jonah, fled from his destiny. He felt himself inadequate to meet the weight of responsibility that lay before him. The revelation was clear and unequivocal, but he was evidently not prepared for it. Instead of rushing forward to the prefigured goal, he shrank backward into himself. His first impulse was towards asceticism. By an irresistible instinct he ran into solitude; "when it pleased God," he says, "to reveal His Son in me, immediately I conferred not with flesh and blood." [1] Writing of the event at a far future day, Paul looks back upon it with a feeling of congratulation; it seems to him that his isolation from the face of his fellow-man had furnished the strongest proof of the originality of his own teaching. So doubtless it had; but that was not Paul's motive for the asceticism. He was not thinking at the time whether he would or would not be esteemed an original teacher; he was trying to postpone the contingency of being a teacher at all. He felt himself depressed by the weight of a great physical calamity, which was to him a moral weight. He felt himself debarred by a thorn, which had come to him as the penalty of past transgression, and he refused, in the meantime, to force his way through the barrier. He fled from the vision of his destiny that he might survey the vision of his own soul.

Whither, then, was he to go? There is a congruity between the mind of the traveller and the scenes which he naturally seeks. What was the natural scene for Paul under these circumstances?

[1] Gal. i. 16.

When a man is intent upon the earthly memories
of the home of Jesus, he goes to Palestine; where
should a man go whose mind is continually dwelling on the memories of Mount Sinai? Clearly to
Arabia.   Accordingly, we are not surprised when,
in the very next sentence of this autobiography, we
read the result of this depressing tendency of an
overwhelming past, "I went into Arabia."[1]   He
went into Arabia because Arabia was already in
his heart.   He sought to realise, in outward vision,
that experience which was present to his soul.   If
asked to speak more definitely, we should say that
he went into Arabia with the hope of expiating his
past.   He thought that if he could stand in the
presence of that awful mountain whose blackness
and lightning and tempest had witnessed in days
of old the promulgation of the Divine law, that if
in that presence he could realise more intensely
and feel more bitterly the weight of his own
nothingness, there might come to him, as to the
prophetess Miriam, a forgiveness of his sin and a
removal of his thorn.   There was a hope in his
heart that, if he could humble himself sufficiently
beneath the mighty power of God, the burden of
that calamity might be lifted which stood in the
meantime as a barrier between himself and his
missionary destiny.   The burden of the calamity
was not what it *was*, but what it indicated; its

[1] Gal. i. 17.

sting was sin. Only by a process of Divine reconciliation, only by a penance which could merit
Divine forgiveness, did the future apostle of the
Gentiles hope to achieve deliverance from his
thorn.

That this desire to win forgiveness by personal
expiation lay at the root of Paul's visit to Arabia,
is evident to me from the fact that his earliest
recorded struggle is one which begins almost immediately after his conversion. I shall call this
the Arabian struggle, to distinguish it from subsequent moral conflicts. It is to the Arabian period
of Paul's life that I assign the first of these three
great strains of mental agony which he has expressed in the words, " for this thing I besought
the Lord thrice that it might depart from me." I
have called it a strain of mental agony, because he
himself, in looking back, virtually calls it a stage of
his Gethsemane. No man can read the passage
without seeing that, at the time when he is recording his three struggles, he has in his mind the scene
of the garden. Not that he thought of this when
he was passing *through* this first struggle. I do
not believe Gethsemane was yet in his mind. He
had begun not with the Christ of the cross, but
with the Christ of the crown. His first acquain-
tance with the Son of man had not been as the
crucified, but as the exalted One. His earliest
vision of Him had been the vision of His resurrec-

tion, of His immortality, of His superiority to the
limits of space and time; his missionary call itself
had been founded upon that vision. His communion with the cross came later, and will be
considered in its due place. But the point for us
to observe in the meantime is how great must have
been the agony of a struggle the memory of which,
long years after, could suggest to Paul's mind one
of the trials in Gethsemane. If, even at that late
day, he could use such a simile to describe it, how
severe must have been the pain at the actual time
of the occurrence! It is not every event which
burns itself into the soul in such a way as to be
reproduced in middle life with undiminished pain.
The Arabian struggle was such an event; it was
Paul's first Christian pain, and first pain is ever
the severest. It was the struggle of a soul to
emancipate itself, by an act of personal expiation,
from the effects of a moral past which had left its
impress upon his physical frame. Into the nature
of that conflict we are not permitted to gaze; history is silent upon its record, and his own confession
has alone revealed it. Doubtless it was a time of
watching and fasting, perhaps of those very watchings and fastings which at a future day he cata-
logued amongst his labours. Earning his bread by
making tents for the Bedouins, he probably took
little bread, and dwelt beneath few tabernacles. In
many vigils under the open sky, in many hours of

prayer amid the storm and rain, in continual self-mortification, in the constant effort to realise his own humility and nothingness,—above all, in the daily crucifixion of that flesh which, because it was the seat of his thorn, had become the memorial of his corruption, he sought to earn the removal of his penalty, and to obtain a liberation from the days of old.

And the result was failure; that, too, helped to render permanently vivid the memory of his pain. A man's first failure is burned more intensely into his soul than his first success. Paul's earliest experience of Christianity was an experience of defeat —of effort futile, of prayer unanswered. How do we know that his first effort was futile? The reason for the assertion is well worth considering. When we read the Epistles to the Galatians and to the Romans, we find that, from beginning to end, their burden consists in ringing the changes on one thought—the impossibility of being justified by law. Where did Paul get that thought? We commonly think of it as a mere dogma or doctrine of his theology. Be it so; but let us remember, at least, that it was a dogma new to the religious world, and discovered for the first time by Paul himself. Where did Paul discover it? If we were asked where Timothy or Titus discovered it, we would have no difficulty in finding for it, in their case, a purely dogmatic origin; we should say at once that

F

they had derived it from Paul. But whence did
Paul derive it? Not from his ancestors; it was
contrary to the spirit of his ancestors,—it was the
very thought which separated him from the home
of his nativity. Is it not clear that it was to him
an independent personal experience? However
much in after-years it crystallised into a dogma,
it was at the beginning a fact of the life. It was
not by dogma that Paul arrived at it; he arrived
at it by stern practical discipline. I have often
remarked that nowhere does he use the singular
number so frequently as in referring to the struggle
to justify one's self by the claims of law. "The law
of the spirit of life hath made *me* free from the law
of sin and death;" "there is a law in *my* members
warring against the law of my mind;" "O wretched
man that *I* am, who shall deliver me from this body
of death?" Why is this? Is it not because Paul
had learned the uselessness of legal penance not
from any mere traditional dogma, but from an experience of living pain? It was to him not a pre-
cept but a memory. It was the memory of that
Arabian struggle in which, for the first time, there
strove together in his heart the old life and the new.
It was the memory of a struggle in which he had
sought by vigils, by fastings, by daily and hourly
humiliations, to wash out the dark stain from the
record of his past, and to purchase by forgiveness
a liberation from its penal thorn. Above all, it was

the memory of a struggle in which he had reaped nothing but weariness, in which his vigils had been vain, his fastings powerless, his humiliations abortive, and which, at the end of the day, left him in possession of his weakness still.

Does Paul now return from Arabia? His experiment at the foot of Mount Sinai has been a failure; does he abandon the search in this direction? Not so; the hour of his failure is but the beginning of a new epoch. If I have rightly interpreted the mental reminiscences revealed in his epistles, there are two periods in his Arabian struggle—the period of Mount Sinai, and what may be called the period of the Sinaitic desert. The period of Mount Sinai was the time of abortive penance, the season in which he stood under the shadow of an avenging law, and failed to find rest from its shadow. But just at this moment there came into the mind of Paul a thought which changed the current of his whole after-life. This law, beneath whose majesty he cowered, had only begun with Mount Sinai; what had been the guide of his countrymen before reaching that mountain? That they had possessed a guide, and a powerful one, was beyond all question. What had led them within the precincts of Arabia? What had conducted them beyond the bondage of Egypt? What had been their sustaining power in the patriarchal days before Egypt? The law had not then been given; Mount Sinai was still in-

visible; the thunderings and the lightnings were
as yet unheard. What was in these days the substitute for law? Paul asked the question, and from
the Jewish scriptures themselves he received a very
surprising answer. They told him that before the
days of law there had been days of promise, that
previous to the deterring by threats there had been
the attracting by rewards. So far was Mount Sinai
from being the origin of Jewish worship, it was a
mark of the decline of that worship. The giving of
the law was an indication not of spiritual strength,
but of spiritual declension; law was "the child
of the bondwoman."[1] The true freedom of the
Jewish nation had from the beginning lain not in
law but in faith, in the prophetic belief of the coming
mercies of God. Not Moses but Abraham had been
the founder of the Hebrew commonwealth, and the
justification of Abraham had been a justification by
faith.[2] Might not he (Paul) go back to that standpoint? Was it necessary that, in becoming a Christian, he should cease to be a Jew? He must, indeed,
cease to be a legalist; but was there not a national
life behind legalism? was not Abraham older than
the law? and was not Abraham justified by faith?
Why should he not go back to Abraham? why
should not the whole nation go back to Abraham?
The law was an excrescence, an after-growth, an
accommodation to passing needs; the original thing

[1] See Gal. iv. 22, and sequel.   [2] See Romans iv. 16, and sequel.

was the promised mercy and the faith in that mercy. Would not the return to this primitive standpoint, instead of being an innovation, be in reality a conservative movement, in which his country would purchase national freedom by retracing her steps into the golden past?

And Paul did go back. His conflict under the shadow of Mount Sinai was the crisis hour between the old life and the new. At the close of that hour he was already loosed from the bonds of Mosaism. But in being loosed from Mosaism he did not all at once pass into Gentilism. There was an intermediate stage between the followers of Moses and the sons of the Gentiles; it was the stage of the children of Abraham. Paul's first Christianity, after leaving Mount Sinai, was a Christianity which had indeed ceased to be Judaic, but only by becoming Hebraic. It was still grounded on the Old Testament, only it was on the Old Testament in its patriarchal age. He accepted justification by faith, instead of justification by law, but his faith was as yet only the faith of Abraham. It was not yet a receptive faculty by which he had communion with Christ; it was simply a prophetic belief in the promised mercy of God through Christ. He said to himself, 'May not God's strength be perfected in my weakness? He has called me to be a missionary, and, morally, I am unfit to be a missionary. I bear about in my body the penalty of a great transgression, and this is itself sufficient to constitute my failure. But was not Abraham himself called to be a missionary when he was physically inadequate ? Did not the glory of his call simply consist in this, that he could only accept it through faith in God's almighty power ? Why should not mine be a similar experience ? Why should not God's power to me be manifested in bearing my moral weakness, just as it was manifested to Abraham in bearing his physical weakness ? If, in spite of his thorn, God made him the instrument in the construction of a great spiritual dominion, why should not His glory be magnified by making me, in spite of my thorn, an instrument in the construction of the kingdom of Christ ?'

Such I believe to have been Paul's thought—the thought which marked the conclusion of his Arabian struggle. Nay, I believe it was even more pointed than this. I think it was at this stage that there entered into his mind an idea which moulded largely his whole after-life. Might not the strength of God be manifested in his weakness not merely negatively but positively, not simply in spite of his thorn, but through his thorn ? Might he not cherish the faith that the mercy of God in Christ would not merely forgive his past, but atone for his past ? Might not the Divine power reveal itself, just by lifting up his own dark deeds into the spiritual order of events, by transmuting his crosses into gold ? He had left on the wayside impediments to the development of the gospel; why should not Divine grace manifest itself by transforming these impediments into the steps of an ascending ladder? Was it not conceivable that, in the plan and purpose of the Highest, his past bad actions should be made to work together for good? They were bad before leaving his hands, but the moment they left his hands, were they not part of God's universe? Had they not ceased to be his after he had done them? How could these deeds of his exist in eternal dualism with the works and ways of God? must not they too be gathered into the Divine mosaic?

What relation in the mind of Paul this hope had to the person of Christ is a question which I shall consider in the next chapter. In the meantime I am simply emphasising the fact that it was a hope, and the first personal hope which Paul had experienced in his new life. The vision of the risen Messiah had revealed to him the prospect of the Christian kingdom; here for the first time he received a prospect for himself. I do not say he had reached the stage of crucifixion to the world which he afterwards attained; that stage is only perfected when a man enters into a new freedom. As yet Paul did not feel free; his only safety lay in an absolute and implicit surrender of his own will to the power of the Highest. His personal life was rather overshadowed and controlled than strengthened and invigorated by its contact with the Divine.

Nevertheless, if his strength as a man had not yet
come, his strength as a missionary had. That strength
was displayed in what may be called his incipient
Calvinism—his determination to put the will of God
in the foreground, and his own will in the background. Rising up from his Arabian struggle, he
prepares to prosecute his missionary calling, and it
is a very remarkable fact that he seeks to prosecute
that calling precisely in those places to which his
nature is most repugnant. As we read his autobiographical narrative of the events which followed
the Arabian sojourn, we cannot fail to be impressed
with the conviction that Paul successively chooses
for evangelistic enterprise precisely those three dis-
tricts where he did not wish to go. His immediate
transition is back to Damascus.[1] It was a voluntary
choice of humiliation—a crucifixion of the natural
man. Damascus had been the scene of his prostration—the scene in which his old life had been
humbled by the arrestive grace of God; it required
Calvinistic courage to begin there. There was a
stern justice in the criminal being led back to the
scene of his crime, that on the very spot he might
undo it — a justice which Paul appreciated, and
which, doubtless, dictated his first missionary course.
He felt it incumbent on him to bear the heat
he had himself created,—to experience the first
torture of that fire which he had been the means

[1] Gal. i. 17.

of kindling.   Damascus was the fitting beginning
for such a life as Paul's, the just commencement
for a heart weighed down with a remorseful past,
and struggling by word and deed to have that past
undone.

And so Paul goes to Damascus, and begins there
to preach that faith which he had formerly sought to
destroy.   By-and-by Damascus casts him out [1]—a
strong testimony to the intensity of his preaching.
The next time the curtain rises there is a change of
scene—he has passed from Damascus into Jerusalem.[2]
It is a second and a deeper humiliation.   If Damascus had been the scene of his crime, Jerusalem had
been the scene of his dignity.   It was associated
with the memories of his Jewish greatness, of that
greatness which had come to him from his support
of the national faith.   It recalled the days when he
had been a Pharisee of the Pharisees, a leader of the
patriotic instincts of his country.   It was a hard
thing to go back there—to go back as a representative of that very party whom he had gained his
reputation by decrying.   A spirit of self-calculation
would have prompted Paul to have delayed such a
missionary journey until he had made a new reputation to counterbalance the loss of the old.   But the
very difficulty of the situation was Paul's motive for
accepting it.   Its attractiveness was its humiliation.
He placed Jerusalem in the foreground, just that he

[1] 2 Cor. xi. 32, 33.   [2] Gal. i. 18.

might taste the full penalty of his past.   He went
there in the days of his deepest contrast with his
former self, just that the outward humiliation of the
contrast might be apparent to his Jewish brethren.
It was an act of social expiation, and as such it was
courted, not shunned.

Then the curtain falls once more, and when it
rises again we are in yet another scene.   Jerusalem
has faded from our view, and we are standing with
Paul in the province of Cilicia.[1]   It is the deepest
humiliation of all.   If Damascus was the scene of
his crime, if Jerusalem was the scene of his dignity,
Cilicia, according to universal tradition, was the scene
of his nativity.   Here had been his home-life; here
had been passed the days of his early development;
here had been formed and ventilated those opinions
of Jewish exclusiveness which had characterised his
after-career.   The opinions of youth are ever expressed with the greatest vehemence, and it is of
all things the most difficult to confess that these
have been wrong.   Paul had left Cilicia burning
with the zeal of his first convictions, and conscious
that these convictions were a matter of notoriety to
the companions of his home-life.   It was a hard
thing, a humiliating thing, to come back after a
few years and tell these companions not only that
his convictions were burnt out, but that they had

[1] Gal. i. 21.

been replaced by contrary fires. It was a hard
thing to be pointed at as an instance of mental
instability, as one who had falsified the expectations
of his youth, and reversed the estimate which the
comrades of his youth had formed. It was the
hardness of the trial that prompted Paul to seek it.
He owed this humiliation to a past which called for
atonement, and he was eager to prostrate his old life
before the feet of infinite justice.

Such is the framework of the first period of Paul's
Christian history ; but it is only the framework.
What is the picture ? We see the man moving
successively through the missionary spheres of
Damascus, Jerusalem, and Cilicia : what is, during
this time, the character of the man himself ? What
is the nature of that first gospel which marks the
opening of his missionary career ? What is his
mental attitude towards the old faith in his earliest
experience of the new ? We have seen that the
moment of his conversion was not immediately accompanied by a sense of moral courage ; still less
should we expect that it would be accompanied by a
fulness of intellectual inspiration. The translation
of Paul into Christianity was the translation into a
new order of thought ; but here, as everywhere else,
the stage of initiation must precede the stage of
completion. What was Paul's stage of intellectual
initiation ? What was the earliest form in which

the objects of Christian thought presented themselves to his gaze, and what was that process of
education by which he first arrived at a knowledge
of these forms?   These are questions which I shall
endeavour to answer in the next chapter.

CHAPTER V.

PAUL'S FIRST GOSPEL: SOURCES OF HIS CHRISTIAN
EDUCATION.

WHAT was the nature of that gospel which marked
the beginning of Paul's missionary life? Was it
universal, or was it particular? Was it an equal
invitation to all the world, or was it tinged as yet
with a certain leaven of Judaism? I believe that
in one sense it was universal, and in another sense
particular. I think that, on the one hand, the vision
of the resurrection Christ had already impressed Paul
with the glorious destiny of the Gentile nations;
yet it seems to me that, at this stage of his history,
he had not wholly emancipated himself from the
trammels of the national faith. We shall therefore take up these aspects one by one. We shall
begin by considering in what sense Paul's gospel
was even now a universal invitation, and we shall
afterwards go on to consider in what sense it
was still bound with the grave-clothes of a dead
past.

And first, Paul had made a discovery. He had
found that in the religion of Judaism the conservative was the true liberal. In the large number of
religious beliefs, the progress of liberal thought is
proportionate to the advance of time; Paul had discovered that in Judaism the order of development
was in the inverse ratio. He had found that, in proportion as he retraced his steps towards a distant
past, the spirit of the Hebrew nation became more
large and charitable,—that in this respect it had the
aspect of a triangle, and was broadest at its base.
The days of Moses had been days of restriction, of
limitation, of narrowness. But when Paul went
back to the age earlier than Moses, when he directed
his view to that patriarchal period in which were
laid the beginnings of the national life, he found
that the beginnings of this life had been marked
by universal aspirations. The horizon which had
stretched before the eyes of Abraham had been an
unlimited horizon. God had taken him out beneath
the stars, and had shown him in a moment of time
all the points of the compass. There had flashed
before his gaze a vision of humanity itself, in its
length and its breadth, its height and its depth.
There had come into his heart the thought of a
universal brotherhood, of a brotherhood which he
owed to man as man, without national distinctions,
and without local limitations. There had entered
into his mind the hope that he himself might be

destined to be a missionary to this universal race, a pioneer of its civilisation, a forerunner of its development. There had risen before his eyes the image of a great deliverer, who was to come from his own loins, and be the fulfiller of his own aspirations,—a hope which expressed itself in the world-wide prophecy, " in thy seed shall all families of the earth be blessed." In this universal promise, in this unlimited aspiration, had the germ of Judaism begun. Its earliest period had been its most catholic; its beginnings had been free, unrestrained, bounded only by humanity. The faith of Abraham, as it appeared to Paul, was the faith in a universal man. It was the belief that, in the fulness of time, there would come forth from his own lineage one whose perfect righteousness would expiate the unrighteousness of all the world,—a life whose untarnished beauty would stand before the face of the Father as an atonement for all in the past which had been unbeautiful, as a vindication and justification of the ancient mandate " let us make man."

Such, in the view of Paul, was the original code of Jewish righteousness. But now, as with earnest heart he ponders the subject, he makes a further and a more remarkable discovery; he finds that, as a matter of fact, this code had never been repealed. He finds that the law of Moses, whatever interpretation might have been put upon it in later times, had never in its origin been designed to supersede

the faith of Abraham.[1] He finds that this law had
been given not as a cure of badness, but as a cure
only of the manifestation of badness—in other words,
of crime. " The law was added because of transgres-
sions."[2] It was imposed upon men not for the purpose of making them righteous, but with the view of
restraining them from deeds of injustice and violence. It was sent to keep man from violating the
rights of man,—to prevent him from leaping the
fences and pilfering from the ground of his brother.
It superseded no code of original righteousness; it
came only to supplement that code when the ideal
of the heart had lost the freshness of its first glow.
It came to invest the present with that sense of
awful majesty which the future had ceased to wear,
and to substitute the fear of a temporal penalty for
that hope of a coming glory which had in the days
of old been adequate to the life of man.

In the view of Paul, then, the law was never
meant to be a guide to moral life. It was only
designed to be a line of boundary between the moral
and the immoral, to consitute a regiment of police
which should prevent the passions of men from
breaking forth into deeds of crime. Accordingly,
it follows that, in the view of Paul, the perfect keeping of the law was by no means equivalent to a
perfect fulfilment of righteousness. I am aware
that I am here at variance with the popular opinion.

[1] Gal. iii. 17.   [2] Gal. iii. 19.

It is commonly thought that, in the view of Paul, the law was introduced just to show man how spotless the righteousness of God was, and how impossible it was that man should keep it. I can only say that in this case the law miserably failed in its design so far as Paul himself was concerned. He certainly regarded the keeping of it as a very easy thing, so easy that, to his mind, the achievement did not indicate any great amount of righteousness at all. He says that he himself was, "touching the righteousness which is in the law, blameless." How could he say that he was blameless? Remember that when he uttered these words he was already a Christian, looking back with dismay upon the days when he was not a Christian. Should we not have expected that he would have stigmatised these days as *full* of blame? Should we not have thought that he would have contrasted the riches of the new state with the pinching poverty of the old? Is it not surprising, then, that in looking back he should have pronounced that old state to be blameless? It would be indeed surprising on the common view that Paul held the righteousness of the law to be a perfect righteousness. But is it not plain from this very passage that he held the reverse? Is it not evident that he means to teach what a miserable standard the righteousness of the law must have been when he himself was able, in looking back even from a Christian standpoint, to feel that he had kept it perfectly,

that, touching its righteousness, he had been blameless? He does not mean to praise himself, but to
indicate how poor must have been a rule of righteousness which should have allowed such a man as he,
not only to believe himself, but actually to *be* blameless according to its requirements.

Such, then, was Paul's position in relation to the
law. He never doubted that a man could keep it
perfectly, never doubted that he himself had fulfilled
it. Its very reproach to him was just the fact that
it *could* be kept by men whose hearts were steeped
in sin. Its defect lay not in its impracticableness,
but in its inadequateness. Paul felt that a man
might be legally blameless, and a deep-dyed sinner
still. He felt that he might keep the law without
even offending in a single point, and be yet at that
very moment in the gall of bitterness, and in the
bond of iniquity. He felt that the conviction of
such a righteousness would never satisfy any man,
had never satisfied the Jew himself. What was the
reason that the best men of his nation had ever been
the most impressed with sin? Why had the dis-
satisfaction always been expressed most loudly by
those who had reached the top of the hill? Was it
not because the revelation was there made that the
top of the hill was not the top of the universe?
Was it not because the conscience of Israel had at
all times been more exacting than its code, and
asserted its claims most strongly just when its code

had been observed? It demanded from man in behalf of God a perfect righteousness, a righteousness which should indeed fulfil the law, but which the law itself could never fulfil. The moral hope of the nation had really rested in an incipient Christianity, had reposed in the aspiration contained in the faith of Abraham, that the latest fruit of the tree of life would atone to the Father for the comparative barrenness of the intermediate branches.

I have now answered the first of the proposed questions—To what extent Paul's new gospel had divorced him from the ancient Judaism? I have arrived at the conclusion that he had reached a liberal attitude by assuming a more conservative position. He had gone back from the legal to the patriarchal age, from the law of Moses to the faith of Abraham. He had found there that the period of the most primitive development had been the period of the most enlarged hope for humanity. The stream had been widest at its source. The aspirations of Judaism had been least narrowed and confined precisely at that stage in which they had begun to be. At that stage Paul stood. He took his stand in the patriarchal period, side by side with Abraham, and he shared the hope of Abraham in the advent of a life whose humanity would be unlimited, and whose blessing would be universal.

Had Paul, then, ceased to be a Jew? Had he

emancipated himself from the last trace of national-
ism ?   Had he now become what he afterwards was
—the apostle of the Gentiles distinctively and un-
qualifiedly ?   It is my opinion that he had not.   He
had passed from Judaism into Hebraism, but there
was one point in which the Hebrew was united
to the Jew.   There was a rite which the age of
legalism had confessedly derived from the patriarchal
age—the ordinance of circumcision.[1]   In accepting
the faith of Abraham, it is natural on the very
surface to suppose that Paul accepted this faith
with all its accompaniments.   He left behind him
as non-essential whatever was of later origin, but he
probably embraced with all the more tenacity every
element of that period from which he had elected to
begin.   Circumcision was one of these elements.
It belonged to the age of Hebraism as distinguished
from that of Judaism.   It was interwoven with the
first universal hope of humanity, was closely associated with the belief that a blessing was reserved
for all mankind.   Would it be surprising if, at the
outset, Paul should have deemed it an essential condition of that blessing ?   Would it be wonderful if
he should have accepted it as incumbent on those
who would be partakers of the faith of Abraham ?
Even in the absence of any further evidence, would
it not be natural to suppose that, in adopting the
universal scope of Abraham's promise, he should

[1] Gen. xvii. 10.

have expected those who embraced it to enter
through Abraham's gate ?

But we are not left without any further evidence.
There are two passages in St Paul's letters which
seem to me to bear directly on this question. The
first of these is expressed in the memorable reminiscence : "Henceforth know we no man after the
flesh : yea, though we have known Christ after the
flesh, yet now henceforth know we Him no more." [1]
The point to be here observed is, that Paul declares
there was a time when he knew Christ after the
flesh ; in other words, when he had a more superficial view of Christianity than that at which he
had then arrived. When was that time of comparative superficialness ? The common interpretation relegates it to the days of Saul of Tarsus.
Paul is supposed to mean that he recognised a
physical Messiah in the period previous to his
adoption of Christianity. I shall waive altogether
the question whether the reference to a time so far
remote is compatible with the words of the passage
before us, whether the phrase " now henceforth "
can legitimately and grammatically be reckoned
equivalent to "for these fourteen years back." Let-
ting that pass, I shall simply ask whether Paul, in
looking back from a Christian standpoint, would
have been likely to have dignified with the name of
Christian knowledge his original reverence for the

[1] 2 Cor. v. 16.

Jewish Messiah. Is it probable that this man, who is conscious that he has received from Christianity a radical change, should, in the very face of that consciousness, have honoured his worship of the national ideal by calling it a knowledge of Jesus of Nazareth? Has he not elsewhere declared that when he became a Christian he held to be loss the things which he had formerly counted gain? Is it compatible with such a declaration that he should have maintained his recognition of the Jewish Messiah to have been identical in kind, and only different in degree, from the knowledge of that Jesus of Nazareth who was now the object of his hope and love?

The truth is, Paul is not here speaking of the difference between his present Christianity and his former Judaism, but of the difference between his present Christianity and the Christianity of his early days. What he says in effect is this — 'I have now arrived at a stage in which I value no man according to his circumcision or his uncircumcision. I admit, indeed, there was a time in which my opinion of circumcision was so high, that I believed it to be the necessary gate even to Christianity itself. That period has now passed away, and I have come to see that a man's acceptance of Christ is altogether unconditioned by the observance of any fleshly ceremony.' But if this is Paul's meaning, it clearly contains a most valuable biographical reminiscence. It tells us in the clearest language that

Paul in emerging from Judaism did not emerge all in a moment, that there was a period of dim dawn between his hour of night and his hour of morning. He left the gate of legalism that he might stand by a wider gate, but the wider gate was still Jewish, and the more liberal standpoint was still national. He desired all men to be made partakers of the privileges of Israel, and he desired that these privileges should be disencumbered from the burdens of the law, but as yet he still held it to be inevitable and imperative that the blessings of the faith of Abraham should come through the door of circumcision.

The second passage which corroborates my view of this subject is the question addressed to a church of Judaic tendencies, " If I yet preach circumcision, why do I yet suffer persecution " ?[1] It is designed to answer a charge of inconsistency, but we have nothing to do with this here. The point on which I wish to lay stress is the phrase, "if I yet preach circumcision." It clearly implies that there was a time when Paul did preach circumcision. When was that time ? The popular view is that Paul is alluding to the period when he was still unconverted to Christianity, that he is recalling the days in which he had stood forth as a defender of the rights of Judaism against the encroachments of the new faith. But, I ask, how could it be said

[1] Gal. v. 11.

that at that time Paul was a preacher of *circum-cision?* Whatever he defended as Saul of Tarsus, it was not the doctrine of circumcision. That doctrine had never been assailed by Christianity, had never been the question on which the new faith had separated from the old. Even at the moment in which Paul was writing this passage, his brother apostles were all believers in circumcision. The new religion had never dreamed for an instant of overturning this rite. Its aim had been rather the realisation than the degradation of Judaism, and it had sought to accomplish its aim rather by enhancing than by disparaging the institutions of the old life. By no stretch of language could Saul of Tarsus be called a preacher of circumcision; in no proper use of language could he be styled a preacher at all. He was a statesman, a councillor, a diplo-matist, a partisan, an advocate, but in no strict sense a religious teacher. His work lay in the Sanhedrim, not in the temple; his genius was politi-cal, his efforts were for the service of the State. The office of preaching was reserved for his Christian consciousness; it had no place in the heart of his Judaism.

We must conclude, then, that when Paul speaks of having at one time preached circumcision, he is speaking of a Christian and not of a Jewish period. He is virtually telling us that, when he first went out from Jerusalem, he did not at once go to

Ephesus, or Corinth, or Rome, but only the length of Mesopotamia. In emerging from the creed of ancient Israel, he did not all at once stray beyond its borders, did not wholly pass the limits of the old tradition. He passed beyond the environments of legalism so far as these professed to be the ultimate standard of morality; he went back from the age of Moses to the freer atmosphere of the age of Abraham, and found in that atmosphere a more healthy respiration; but he still attached himself and his Christianity to an institution of that age which was purely ceremonial, and he was still unable to dissociate the universal hope from the national rite of circumcision.

I have now answered the two questions proposed at the beginning of this chapter. I have indicated to what extent the gospel of Paul was as yet universal, and to what extent it was still limited and particular. The result has been to establish the position that the Christian illumination of Paul was a process of education,—a process by which he proceeded step by step from the knowledge in part to the knowledge in full. This, accordingly, seems now the proper place to inquire what were the sources of Paul's Christian education. One would imagine beforehand that he had peculiar facilities for such an education. True, he had been born a little out of due time; he had not been an actual spectator of the life and work of the Master. Yet in the

strictest sense he was a contemporary of that life
and work.   His years probably ran nearly parallel
to the years of Jesus.   The disciples of Christianity's
dawn were still alive and active, and we have
evidence from Paul's own epistles that they were
accessible to his intercourse.   Under these circumstances we should expect that Paul would have
immediately proceeded to fill up the blanks in his
own Christian knowledge by a reference to contemporary experience.   His vision of Christ had been
only a vision of the closing drama, and precisely of
that stage of the drama where the scene was transferred from earth to heaven.   The first step of Paul's
education must clearly be the filling up of the earthly
blank in his knowledge of the Son of man.   His
vision had been only that of a resurrection Christ ;
his earliest journey must be a retracing of his steps
into those human scenes which preceded the resurrection.   In seeking a knowledge of that past, should
we not have expected that Paul would have gone
directly and immediately to the living sources of
tradition ?   Should we not have thought that, in
the very presence of contemporaries whose memory
was charged with the personal incidents of the
Master's life, he would have hastened at once to
supply the vacancy by seeking from these a first-
hand portrait of Jesus ?   It seems at first sight of
all things the most natural that Paul, in his earliest
search for the human memories of Christ, should

have drawn his information from that band of primitive disciples who had been with Him from the beginning, and had followed Him to the end.

And yet we must confess that in this matter we are doomed to experience a surprise. In point of fact Paul's earliest resort for information is not to contemporary sources. Desirous as he must have felt to supply that which was lacking in his knowledge of the earthly life of Jesus, he does not immediately repair to those streams of living tradition from which at once the want could have been compensated. On the contrary, his immediate resort is to the Old Testament. His resurrection vision had told him that Jesus was the Messiah: instead of inquiring what this Messiah had actually been, he immediately proceeds to inquire what He *must* have been. He does not repair, as we should naturally expect, to the living voices of Peter, James, and John, but to the prophetic voices of Isaiah, Hosea, and the Psalmist. He wants to know, not so much what really happened as what the Scriptures predicted would happen. In his earliest epistles we look in vain for any historical reminiscence of the man Christ Jesus. Neither in the two letters to the Thessalonians, nor in the single letter to the Galatians, do we find the slightest reference to the daily life of the Christ of Palestine. It is only when he comes to write to the Corinthians that we discover unmistakable evidence of his sympathy

with the historical tradition.   His proofs of the
resurrection Christ embrace a circumstantial narrative of facts which could only have been learned
from contemporaneous sources; but even here it
would be too much to say that it was *based* on
these facts.   On the contrary, we are continually
surprised to find that the main stress of Paul is laid
upon the proof that Christ was raised " according to
the Scriptures."   We marvel at the tenacity and at
the pertinacity with which he reiterates the assertion; and from our modern point of view, we wonder
at the importance with which he invests it.   We
want to hear about the five hundred by whom Jesus
was beheld simultaneously; we want to know what
manner of men they were, and with what degree of
emphasis they asserted their conviction.   It is rather
damping under these circumstances to be perpetually
directed to a remote past, and told to find our comfort in the fact that He was raised " according to the
Scriptures."

Yet a deeper reflection will convince us that,
however unnatural all this seems, it is only unnatural from our point of view.   If we throw ourselves back from the nineteenth century into the
first, we shall find that Paul's conduct in this matter
is not only free from artificialness, but is the genuine
impulse of a spontaneous human nature.   For, let
us consider the difference between the religious
standpoint of the first and nineteenth centuries.   In

our age the objection to Christianity is its miraculousness ; in Paul's age the objection to Christianity was its seeming unscripturalness. The opposing element in the mind of Paul was not the supposed violation of nature's law involved in a Messiah rising from the dead; it was the apparent verdict of the Old Testament that the Messiah could not be dead at all. To the mind of his countrymen, originally to the mind of himself, the notion of a suffering Messiah was at variance with that will of God which was expressed in the Jewish scriptures, and which to him was synonymous with the law of nature. When therefore Christianity presented itself, his first and foremost question was, What did the Bible say ? He did not ask whether it would violate the laws of the physical universe ; that was to him a subordinate consideration. His immediate concern was whether it would violate that order of Divine prophecy which had permeated like a thread the contents of the Old Testament, and had constituted to the heart of Israel the most unchangeable thing in the universe.

Let me illustrate the feeling by a familiar experience of modern life. There is a widespread belief in some quarters that there are at the present day certain spiritual manifestations revealed through the movements of certain articles of furniture. If the evidence for this belief were to be estimated simply by the number of those who have professed to witness the manifestation, it would be as demonstrable as any proposition of Euclid. Measured by such a standard, the "five hundred brethren at once" would be nowhere; the testimony for this later miracle embraces not hundreds but thousands. And yet, the large majority of professing Christians would never dream of even examining one of the witnesses; they would, and actually do, reject the testimony without inquiry. Why? Simply because the thing which is attested appears to them to be at variance with the doctrine of the Bible. They would deem it impiety to take into a moment's consideration any of those outward circumstances which seem to make for or against the theory, because they are convinced beforehand that, if the theory were proved, the Old and New Testaments would be disproved. It is no opposition to the miraculous that prompts the ordinary Christian to foreclose this question of modern spiritualism. Every Christian believes in something equally miraculous, and miraculous, moreover, in a somewhat similar direction. The Catholic recognises the truth of transubstantiation, the belief that the Divine Spirit can transmute itself into material elements; the Protestant, without accepting a transmutation, equally coincides in the conclusion that the Divine Spirit can manifest itself in these material elements. It is therefore no sense of supernaturalism that repels the Christian consciousness from the modern belief in the manifestation of spirits through material forms. It is the Christian consciousness itself that constitutes the ground of the repulsion. It is the belief that the new life is opposed to the old, the conviction that the modern form of revelation would contradict in its earthliness and compromise in its humanness those lofty and Divine precepts which have descended from the spirit of Christianity.

Let us apply this to Paul. Previous to his conversion, he was told on every hand that there had appeared in the heart of the Jewish theocracy a series of new spiritual manifestations. Paul did not make the slightest effort to test the reality of these; he decided beforehand and in advance that they could not be real. His reason for this decision was not any sense of scientific uniformity. He had no objection to a miracle, and was quite ready to admit any alteration in the law of nature, provided it did not touch the first link of the chain. That first link of the chain was to him the will of God, as revealed and expressed in the pages of the Old Testament. But then, in the view of Paul these new spiritual manifestations did touch the first link of the chain; they seemed to him to be at variance with the prophecies of the Old Testament. Such a consideration was sufficient to his mind to decide the case at once. No amount of external testimony would have warranted the acceptance of statements whose acceptance would con-

tradict the verdict of the Jewish Scriptures. Even
if such statements had been verified, it would have
availed them nothing. To the mind of the Jew
there were in existence undoubted facts, which were
with equal undoubtedness to be refused admission
into the mind of man—facts which had their origin
in a power which was not Divine, and their place in
an economy which was founded on other laws from
those of truth.

By-and-by Paul was converted, not by the force
of external testimony, but by the force of a sub-
jective and personal experience. Even then, however, the difficulty which had presented itself to
the anti-Christian leader continued to present itself
to the Christian missionary. The main obstacle to
be combated as an apologist was precisely that
obstacle which originally had made him an opponent. He had been so inveterate a Judaiser
that the habit survived his entrance into Christianity. On the threshold of his new call, it never
occurred to him that the question of his opponents
could be any other than this, " Where is Abel, thy
brother," what have you done with the Old Testament ? It was a sense of that question that drove
him at the outset, not into Jerusalem, but into
Arabia, not towards the scene of the new manifestations, but into the region of the ancient covenant.
He communed not with flesh and blood, just because
flesh and blood could not give the testimony he

desired. He wanted not the testimony of the present but the witness of the past; he was in search, not of facts to corroborate the words of men, but of something to harmonise the words of men with the word of God.

This explains the seeming waste which, from an educational point of view, is involved in Paul's Arabian journey. It seems to the reader as if, even from his own standpoint, he must have been consciously losing time; was it not like going to a school of mathematics for the purpose of learning music? Undoubtedly; but it so happened that Paul could not begin to learn music without a knowledge of the mathematics. He was deeply impressed with the beauty and the inherent harmony of the Christian principle, but he wanted to know that the Christian principle was itself in a straight line with the principles of his fathers. He wanted to ascertain for purposes of defence what he had formerly denied for purposes of aggression—the unity between the new covenant and the old, the conformity of the life of Jesus to the prophetic will of God.

It was when Paul emerged from Arabia, it was when he came forth into the vicinity of Gentile scenes, that he began to feel the inadequacy of his method. To begin his defence of Christianity by a study of the Old Testament was a fitting course for a missionary to the Jews; was it the fitting

H

course for the Apostle of the Gentiles? Was it not
clear that to them the main subject of inquiry was
not the consistency but the *veracity* of the alleged
facts,—not their congruity with the Old Testament,
but their compatibility with human experience?
Paul felt that it was so. He felt that his previous
method had been one-sided, adapted only to a class.
He desired to adapt Christianity to the other class—
those for whom he felt himself specially destined.
But how was he to accomplish this? The new
method clearly demanded a new training. His
knowledge of the Old Testament was an advantage among the Jews; it could contribute nothing
to his success among the Gentiles. To succeed
amongst them, he must go to school not with his
fathers but with his brethren. He must consult
his contemporaries who had been the contemporaries
of Jesus. He must learn from eye and ear witnesses
what had been the actual history of that life of
which he had been only permitted to see the ideal
glory.

And this leads me to counteract an impression
which prevails extensively in Christian circles—that
Paul professed to have derived his information concerning the events of Christ's life from supernatural
sources. The opinion is based upon the passage in
Galatians i. 11-16, in which Paul lays claim not
only to an originality of thought, but to an originality in the mode of its communication. He declares

that the gospel which he preached was neither after the manner of man, nor received from man, that it had come to him directly and immediately from the revelation of God. The natural inference has been that Paul here professes to have received a knowledge of the gospel history without the aid of history,— a record of the life and acts of Jesus without any medium to record them. But, however natural be the inference, the thought is highly unnatural. Are we to suppose that Paul received facilities for obtaining a knowledge of the life of Jesus which were not received by those whose actual commission was to write that life? The third evangelist, in the preface to his gospel, is not ashamed to confess that his knowledge of the life of Jesus was based upon sources not supernatural but natural,—that he was inspired to write his narrative by the fact that others had written on the same theme, and that he was in possession of traditions derived from the earliest contemporary witnesses. Are we to suppose that Paul, whose mission was not that of a biographer but of a preacher, should have deemed himself beyond the necessity of consulting those records of the time which the third evangelist had made the basis of his sacred history?

But the truth is, Paul makes no such claim. In the passage from Galatians which seems to express the claim, he is speaking not of a gospel history, but of a gospel call. The message which he professed to

have received by an original channel was not the
account of Christ's life, but the revelation of Christ's
universality. One has only to read the passage in
order to be convinced of this. Strictly speaking, the
originality to which Paul lays claim is an originality
of ordination. He says, " When it pleased God to
reveal His Son in me, that I might preach Him
among the heathen, immediately I conferred not
with flesh and blood." He means to say that his
commission to preach the equal privileges of the
Gentiles was not a commission derived from any
authority delegated to him by the original apostles;
it came to him by a direct act of Divine ordination
which had made him one of their number, and had
placed him in a position as independent as their
own. He had been the first to receive a revelation
of the universal scope of Christianity, and he had
received that revelation by a communication of the
Divine Master equally direct, though not equally
visible. He had been set apart to his specially
apostolic work by a special act of priestly consecration, and that act of priestly consecration had been
performed in his inner spirit by a hand and by a
voice impalpable to the earthly sense.

And this explains what otherwise would be in-
explicable in the reasoning of Paul's argument in
this chapter of Galatians. On the popular view
that Paul intended to lay claim to a supernatural
communication of the gospel facts, how are we to

account for such words as these? "After three years I went up to Jerusalem to see Peter, and abode with him fifteen days. But other of the apostles saw I none, save James the Lord's brother." [1] Does he mean to imply that the fact of having only seen two contemporaries was a proof that he had received his facts supernaturally? If so, Paul was on this occasion singularly illogical and wonderfully unlike himself. In order to obtain a natural knowledge of the gospel facts, he only required to meet precisely those two persons whom by his own admission he did meet. The whole length and breadth of the earthly life of Jesus was compassed by their testimony. Or will it be said that the strength of his argument lies in the shortness of that period during which he abode with Peter? I must reply that, if his design was merely to avoid the imputation of receiving facts by natural means, the time of his abiding was much too long. Fifteen hours would have been amply sufficient to have put him in full possession of all the salient features of the gospel history; fifteen minutes would have sufficed to have thoroughly established in his mind a conviction that the faith in Christianity rested upon a purely historical basis. If Paul's motive was to suggest the inference that he had received no outward knowledge of the facts because he had only seen two disciples, he managed to suggest an inference of precisely the opposite intent.

[1] Gal. i. 18, 19.

But the case is very different if we suppose his object to have been the proof of his independent ordination. Two of the original apostles could very easily have taught him; two could never have ordained him to the apostolic office. From the historical narrative of the Acts we gather that the apostolic brethren were in the habit of supplying vacancies left in their ranks, but we learn from the same narrative that the vacancy was supplied by the brethren as a whole. If Paul had been set apart for his apostolic work merely by the delegated authority of the original apostles, his own position is that he must have received that authority from a general conclave of all the apostles together, whereas in point of fact, previous to obtaining such a position, he had only seen two of them. He had never been in a situation in which he could receive the hands of the presbytery. He had never met in conclave with those original disciples of the Lord from whose united assembly, and from whose combined will, could alone come an ordination to the apostolic office. The circumstance that he had only seen two was an incontrovertible evidence that, whencesoever he derived his authority to be an apostle, he did not and could not derive it from the will of man.

It is in this light that we must interpret another passage in which Paul seems to lay claim to a supernatural avenue for the attainment of historical knowledge. I allude to the passage, 1 Corinthians

xi. 23, in which, speaking of the Lord's Supper, he says, " I have received of the Lord that which also I delivered unto you, that the Lord Jesus the same night in which he was betrayed took bread." Paul is here commonly supposed to mean that the historical fact of the institution of the Supper was communicated to him in a manner unhistorical, and by a process supernatural. The original disciples learned it through their actual presence at the scene; Paul was not present at the scene, and therefore on this matter he had no direct historical testimony. Under these circumstances it would have seemed the most natural course to get the historical evidence next best — to consult the testimony of those who had been so present. Paul, however, is supposed to be stating that he scorned such subservience. He is supposed to indicate that he had received an account, through a supernatural channel, of those precise words of institution which had fallen upon the natural ear of the original disciples.

A thought more grotesque, an idea more incongruous with the spirit of the New Testament in general, and with the spirit of Paul in particular, was perhaps never conceived. It is contrary to every analogy, contrary to the whole Divine economy. The New Testament emphasises the parsimony of miracles, and disparages the use of wonderful signs; Paul, throughout the whole course of his epistles, never alludes to one such individual sign

as occurring in his own experience.   But if we look
at the matter in the light of Paul's claim to apostolic
ordination, it all becomes clear.   The original disciples had prided themselves on the fact that they
had received the Lord's Supper from the Master's
own hand.   Paul denies that in this respect he is
one whit behind them : " I too have received of the
Lord that which I have delivered unto you."   He is
not speaking, as I take it, of the words of institution
at the sacrament, but of the sacrament itself.   He
says that no contrast can be drawn between his
apostolic ordination and that of the original disciples on the ground of intercourse with the Master.
He claims as immediate an intercourse with the
Master as ever they possessed.   He refuses to admit
that their first participation in the Lord's Supper
enjoyed any privilege which had not equally been
granted to him.   If they had received the sacred
elements from the Master's own hands, so had he.
If they had listened to the Master's own voice in
the words of original institution, so had he.   If they
had recognised the Master's actual presence in the
holy feast, so had he.   He was conscious that when
he had first participated in that bread and wine, he
had been as really and truly in contact with Jesus
as those who had heard His voice and seen His form
on the shores of the Galilean lake.   The ordination
which he claimed was a priesthood after the order of
Melchisedec—a priesthood which he had derived from

no second-hand source, but from the actual touch and impact of the Divine life itself; and it was to emphasise this conviction that he uttered the words to the Church of Corinth, "I have received of the *Lord* that which also I delivered unto you."

We arrive, then, at this conclusion, that Paul's claim to originality was the claim not to an independent channel for the communication of facts, but to an independent channel for the receiving of ordination. At no time does Paul profess to have obtained a knowledge of facts in any other than a natural way. At the stage where we have now arrived he wanted above all things to obtain such a knowledge. He was beginning to find that the conformity of the gospel history to the prophecies of the Old Testament, however powerful an argument it might be with the Jew, had no value whatever with the Gentile. The Gentile demanded a proof for that alleged history itself. Where was Paul to get such a proof? He never dreamed of getting it supernaturally; it was clear to him that, if it came at all, it must come through the medium of contemporaneous testimony. Accordingly, we are not surprised to find that it is to such testimony Paul makes his earliest appeal in the sphere of his Gentile apostleship. We learn from the passage already quoted from Galatians that his first visit to Jerusalem after his Arabian struggle, was a visit just to those two men who, of all others, were best

adapted to satisfy such a need—Peter and James.
It was not merely as leaders of the Christian Church
that Paul sought their intercourse; they were only
leaders of the Christian Church because they had
been contemporaneous witnesses of leading incidents
in the life of the Master. The incidents to which
they witnessed were not identical; the testimony of
the one supplied what was lacking to the other.
The witness of Peter ranged over the days of the
Master's manhood; the witness of James embraced
the period of His early youth. Peter had been with
Him from the opening ministry on the shores of
Galilee to the closing scene in the Garden of Gethsemane; James had been with Him ere ever that
ministry had begun, and had been a spectator of
His life around the family altar. These two lives
were precisely the medium through which Paul's
Christian education required to travel. He had
begun, as we have seen, at the closing stage of the
Master's history. His first introduction to Christianity had been precisely on that spot where the
earthly eyes of the earliest disciples had bidden it
farewell. Paul had begun where they ended—with
the scene of resurrection. His first impression had
been a sense of Christianity's Divine power; it was
necessary that he should move backwards to take up
that humanity which he had left behind. He had
seen the ideal Christ, but he had not yet beheld the
earthly man. That vision he could never behold in

the flesh; he must receive it on trust from those who had been companions of His human way. Where could he better receive it than from the testimony of those two lives which, when taken together, embraced both the man and the child—the life of him who had followed the Master on the sea of human trouble, and the life of him who, on the shores of Galilee, had witnessed the development and the dawn?

CHAPTER VI.

PAUL'S SECOND STRUGGLE AND ITS RESULT.

PAUL, as we have seen, had immediately after his conversion to Christianity experienced a great struggle in Arabia. We have pointed out that it was the conflict rather of the missionary than of the man. It came from the sense of incongruity between his conviction of an apostolic call and his experience of a physical thorn. He recognised the thorn as a mark of the Divine displeasure, and the problem in his mind was to determine how, with the evidence of such displeasure branded on his forehead, he could go forth as missionary to the Gentiles. His Arabian struggle was the effort of his soul to experience a liberation from his thorn— not by reason of his thorn's physical pain, but on account of its moral significance. He wanted to feel that he went forth in the eyes of the heathen accompanied by the unblemished favour of God, and without any outward mark to indicate the presence of God's disfavour.

The result of that struggle we have seen. It ended rather in a passive than in an active resignation. It did not bring Paul to his subsequent stage of glorying in tribulation; it only brought him to a state of mental quietude. He yielded himself up to the mighty power of God. He surrendered himself to the thought that this power might be magnified through the very weakness of its instrument, and that the very hindrance which his thorn undoubtedly presented to missionary success might serve still further to manifest the Divine glory. When Paul therefore emerged from Arabia, it was in the state of one who had experienced a restraining influence upon his sorrow. That sorrow had not been turned into joy, but it had been compelled to sleep. It had been forced to remain quiescent beneath the sense of a Divine all-ruling Will, whose purposes admitted of no scrutiny, and from whose acts there could be no appeal.

But now I must observe that Paul himself never regarded his Arabian struggle as anything more than the initial stage of his conflict. He says of his thorn, in words more than once already referred to, " I besought the Lord thrice, that it might depart from me." The words seem to me to indicate that, to the retrospective experience of Paul, the struggle of his spiritual life embraced three distinct stages, comprehended three successive battle-fields in which he contended with the old enemy for different issues. The first of these conflicts is the Arabian struggle already described. As we have said, it was a struggle rather of the missionary than of the man. It was the effort of Paul to reconcile his call to apostleship with a sense of that ceremonial uncleanness which had been hitherto deemed a barrier to the service of the sanctuary. That battle-field had been won; the conscience of Paul had triumphed by putting itself under the will of the Highest. But, clearly, the victory which had been gained was as yet a very small one. The struggle which the apostle had experienced was only his struggle *as* an apostle. It was rather official than personal. It was awakened by the contrast between that work of grace which he was required to perform for others and that mark of Divine disfavour which he felt existing in himself. But sin has never perfectly revealed its sting until it reveals itself to the man as a man. Hitherto the personal life of Paul had been somewhat veiled from his sight by the appalling sense of his apostolic mission. It was comparatively easy to lull that storm to rest. From the standpoint of the Divine agency, the defectiveness or the perfectness of the human instrument was a matter of indifference; in the work of the apostleship God was all in all. But it was a very different matter when sin confronted the *man,*—when the problem before him was not how he should succeed in his work, but how he should be right in his conscience. Such a question, in the very nature of the case, cannot be solved by an appeal to the absolute power of God. The sphere of conscience is precisely that sphere where God elects not to be absolute, precisely that region in which He leaves a margin to the creature's will. When the problem confronts a man in this direction, he requires to battle it out on human grounds, to weigh the testimony of his own heart, to wrestle with himself until the breaking of the day. Such was to be Paul's second struggle. He was to meet with the shadow of his former self, to see it no longer through a mere official veil, but face to face and man to man. He was to confront the spectacle of sin as sin—not in its ceremonial uncleanness, not in its liability to punishment, not in its disadvantageous consequences to a Christian apostle, but simply and solely in the unrest it occasions to a human mind.

I have called Paul's first conflict the Arabian struggle, because its sphere was Arabia. Perhaps I shall not be far astray if I call his second conflict by the name of the Antiochian struggle. If Arabia was the scene of his Judaic Christianity, Antioch was probably the spot where his Judaism received its first serious check. That city was rapidly becoming the new centre of the Christian life. Jerusalem, which had been the parent stream of the Christian faith, was beginning to be left behind as the river of that faith broadened its banks. The

shadow of the temple worship was receding, and the
ark of the new covenant was being transplanted into
another scene.   That scene was Antioch.   There
was no spot in the world more unlike in every particular to the associations of Jerusalem.   Jerusalem
was the scene of unity; Antioch was the place of
variety.   Jerusalem revealed the necessity for a
rigid agreement; Antioch displayed the impossibility of imposing such a concord.   Jerusalem had
room only for one phase of belief; Antioch was, by
the very nature of its population, the sphere of
many minds.   Into this sphere Christianity had
come at the very moment when Paul was passing
through his first experience of struggle.   The followers of Jesus were founding a new capital—a
capital which was to be a more powerful centre
for Christianity than ever Jerusalem had been for
Judaism.   Its comparative power was to lie in its
comparative liberality.   It was a soil fitted by its
very nature to receive all manner of seeds, and to
nourish growths of vastly different kinds.   To plant
Christianity there, was already to transplant it, to
modify it, to enclose it in a new environment.   It
was impossible henceforth that it should ever be
the rigid, narrow, monotonous thing which it had
been in days of old.   It was inevitable that it
should become less Jewish and more human, and
it was specially inevitable that the rite of circumcision, which had constituted a part of its original

bond of fellowship, should be superseded and suppressed by the bond of Christian love.

We find, both from the narrative in the Acts and
from the testimony of the epistles, that, within a few
years of his conversion, Paul had already become
part of the new Christian centre at Antioch. The
significance of this fact for Paul, as well as for the
other disciples, cannot be overrated. It was the
entrance into a different atmosphere — an atmosphere rather larger than purer. It embraced, as we
have seen, greater varieties of mind, but for that
very reason it embraced greater susceptibilities to
evil. Jerusalem had been a sphere of restrained
vices. The heart of man there was no better than
elsewhere ; but there it was prevented from revealing itself as elsewhere. It was under the dominion
of law, and of a law so rigid as to extend to the
minutest details of human action. But the soil of
Antioch was essentially lawless. It was a sphere
in which man had cast off all restraint, and had
abandoned himself to the impulse of his own will.
Nowhere, perhaps, in the lawless Gentile world had
the spirit of licence taken so deep a hold. The
passions of men seemed to have broken loose.
Licentiousness, profligacy, immorality in every form,
was rampant. All the bands of restraint by which
religion imposes a fetter upon human vices had been
long since rent asunder, and a specimen was given to
the world of human nature in a state of spontaneous

I

freedom.   There could be no more fitting sphere in
which to demonstrate the utter futility of the rite
of circumcision as a moral educator of mankind.
Hitherto human nature had not been seen in its
strength by the Christian disciples; it had been seen
only in that state of repression to which it had been
reduced by a long subjection to law.   Circumcision
had got the credit of effecting more than it really
did; it had been thought to subdue the passions
which were already more than half conquered.   But
here, in this soil of Antioch, the case was very different.   The passions of men were untamed, and the
hearts of men were unaccustomed to control.   What
could a rite or ceremony do against the force of such
a stream ?   It could only manifest its own impotence
in the fact of being swept away.   In the spectacle
of human nature overflowing its embankments at
Antioch, the Christian disciple must have awakened
for the first time to the utter inadequacy and in-
competence of Jewish ceremonialism, must have
perceived for the first time how powerless to the
salvation of the Gentiles was that ancient sacrament of circumcision, which had been for ages the
symbol of admission into the national communion.

I am far from thinking, however, that in the
abandonment of the rite of circumcision, Paul was
merely or even mainly influenced by his geographical
surroundings.   Doubtless on him, as on others, the
vehemence of human vices at Antioch produced a

powerful sense that there was wanted a stronger than any physical restraint. But it seems to me that the ice of his Judaism was broken, not so much by looking on the sins of others as by a sudden awakening to the sense of his own. If it be asked why I regard Paul's awakening to the sense of personal sin as an event contemporaneous with his entrance into Antioch, I must reply that I believe his personal conviction of sin to have reached its intensest form only subsequently to the visit to Jerusalem alluded to in the previous chapter. The earliest revelation which Paul received was, as we have seen, not so much one of human guilt as of human equality. His first perception had been that of the risen Christ, and his vision of the risen Christ had mainly and primarily suggested only the claims of the Gentiles. In order to awaken Paul into a sense of personal sin, it was necessary that he should go back over that road which the original disciples had first travelled. He had only seen the Christ in His form of Divine exaltation; it was necessary that he should see Him in His form of earthly lowliness. His Christian education required, as we have said, to be a regress, a stepping backward over untrodden ground. Christ had only been brought before him in a superhuman aspect; he had to retrace his way into the scenes of His human ministry. He entered into these scenes for the first time when he went up to see Peter at Jerusalem. In his intercourse with that disciple, and in his intercourse with the Lord's brother, he came into his earliest contact with the man Christ Jesus. It was no longer an apparition in the clouds, it was no longer a light of supernatural radiance,—it was a human soul revealing the beauty of humanity, and revealing that beauty through the laws of natural development. In his intercourse with those brethren who had been with the Master in the days of His earthly struggle, Paul must have received his first impression of the inherent loveliness and the sublime sacrificial strength of the human life of Jesus.

Now there is no truth more intuitively certain than the fact that such a vision is necessary to a man's sense of sin. It is a great mistake to imagine that any man can recognise himself to be living in a valley merely by being in the valley. He only comes to recognise the vale by having his eye cast upon the mountain; it is from the sense of height that he receives his impression of lowliness. And what is true in the world of nature, is true in the world of mind. It is equally true both in the intellectual and in the moral sphere. No man can arrive at a sense of his own ignorance except by receiving some rudiments of human knowledge; no man can arrive at a conviction of his own sinfulness except by coming into contact with a higher and a purer life. It is from the sight of moral beauty alone that a man can awaken to the conviction of his spiritual deformity; it is only from the vision of light that he can recognise the presence of his darkness. These are truths as experimentally certain as any mathematical axiom, and it is in their light that we ought to interpret the historical sequence of Paul's spiritual experience. His vision of his own inherent depravity ought to be dated from his vision of the human loveliness of the Son of man. That vision only came to him in the day when the human life opened upon him, when he made a step backward from the Christ on the plains of Damascus to the Christ on the shores of Galilee. It took its rise from that visit to Jerusalem in which he came into personal contact with those who had both seen and handled the word of life, and was brought into personal fellowship with the immediate disciples of the Lord. Amid the solitudes of Arabia he had only communed with the Christ of supernatural power; in the companionship with Peter and James he received his first impressions of the moral strength and beauty of the Christ of history.

And with that vision he received at the same time his first impressions of his own moral turpitude. The sight of supernatural glory cannot awaken in man a sense of human degeneracy. Nothing but a *human* loveliness can impress a human soul with its own sin. It is from the vision of the human Christ, imparted during the fifteen days in Jerusalem, that I date the beginning of that personal struggle which left such a prominent impress on the apostle's future life. The nature of that struggle will be found delineated in the seventh chapter of Romans. I have no doubt whatever that, although written in the present tense, this chapter is, and is intended to be, a biographical record. I do not read it as a statement of what was passing in the apostle's mind at the time when he wrote the epistle, but as a narrative of what passed through his mind in the days when he was first awakened to the sense of the awful contrast between himself and the Son of man. He expresses it as a present experience, to indicate the vividness with which it still lived in his thoughts. It had left its imperishable marks upon him. Its memory was as fresh and green as if it had happened yesterday. As he thought of it, it seemed to him as if he were living over the struggle again—reproducing the pain of the old conflict, and undergoing the mental crucifixion of former years; and he expressed this sense of vividness by transforming the history into a description, and depicting the past experience as an event of the present hour.

Let it be observed that in the very heat of this mental struggle Paul never for a moment loses sight of the fact that the struggle itself was the result of a higher and not of a lower life; he says that sin assumed to him its fearful appearance, and worked

in him the sense of death " by that which is good." [1]
He never for a moment doubts that his pain is the
fruit of a higher joy, that his perception of the
valley comes from the sight of a mountain. That
which has awakened him to the vision of his own
deformity is itself a vision of beauty; it is Christ
alone that has shown to him his distance from
Christ. He has become the partaker of what might
be called a double consciousness. There are two
lives within him—one pointing to the heavens, and
the other to the earth; and in the conflict of these
two lives, he feels as if he were two men. But he
never forgets the fact that the lower or earthly man
has only come into consciousness by reason of the
higher or heavenly one; the birth of the Christ
within him has alone revealed the life of the first
Adam. The higher life is to Paul his real self, the
lower life is his imprisonment. His higher life has
been born in a dungeon, and has come to the recognition of its chains. It feels itself to be in a
position which it has no right to occupy. There is
a contradiction between its will and its power of
performance; it desires to be free, but its fetters
impede its way. It has aspirations toward the true
and good, but they are destroyed when they touch
the chains of the prison-house. Paul has awakened
to the sense of a deep antagonism in his own nature,
—an internecine war between two lives which are

[1] Rom. vii. 13.

striving for the mastery, and struggling for mutual extermination. His most prominent impression is a sense of utter helplessness, "Who shall deliver me from this body of death?" He is more impressed with his helplessness than with his unworthiness. He feels that in the inner man he does delight in the law of God, and that, if left to his true self, he would be pure. He cries out for something to put him in a normal position, to restore him to his native freedom, to give him the right and the power to breathe his natural air; and the deepest grief of his soul proceeds from his perception that, in spite of the strength of his own desire, he is himself utterly unable to realise the aspiration of his heart.

Now, it is from this sense of helplessness that I date the first step of Paul's real departure from Judaism. His first real departure from Judaism was not his acceptance of Christianity; neither he nor his Christian contemporaries ever dreamed that in embracing the faith of Jesus they were surpassing the faith of Israel. The beginning of Paul's rupture with Judaism was his rejection of the doctrine of circumcision. We have seen that Paul's Christianity had indeed produced a change in his attitude towards the national religion, but it was a change in the direction of conservatism; he had only gone back from the legal to the patriarchal. When he emerged from Arabia, he was still an adherent of the faith of Abraham, and still held that the main portal into the temple was the gate of circumcision. But as he drew near to Antioch, and heard the diverse voices of many minds, he began to ask if this one gate would suit them all. As he drew nearer still, and beheld the unrestrained vices of many hearts, he began to ask if, even when admitted, this one gate would be fit to hold them in. Above all, as he turned his eye inwards upon that Jerusalem experience which he had gathered by the way,—as he thought of the new and human vision which he had received of Christ's beauty from his fellowship with the primitive disciples, and as, by reason of that vision, there rose within him as there had never risen before, a sense of his personal deformity, he began to ask for the first time the most solemn question of all—Was the gate sufficient for himself?

The answer to that question was not difficult. It was impossible that Paul, when once awakened to a sense of the vehemence of the old life within him, could ever imagine that it could be restrained by such an embankment as circumcision. But if so, what then? If circumcision was not fitted to be an aid in restraining the passions of Christians, had it a right to have any place at all within the Christian system? If it was not calculated to be a gate of restraint, what claim could it have to be a gate of entrance? Were not the passions of the heart the result of a fleshly or carnal element? How could a carnal element be expelled by that which was itself carnal ?   Was not circumcision simply a ceremony of the flesh, and as such, how could it have any power over the spirit ?   Had there not been an error in retaining this old gate of Judaism ?   Were not the limits even of Arabia too narrow to be a basis for the creed of Christendom ?   Had not the time come in which it would be desirable to widen the portals of the Christian Church, and to admit future adherents within her pale upon larger and more spiritual grounds ?

It is from this period that I date the beginning of what may distinctively be called Paul's Gentile life. I say the beginning.   I shall presently show that the Gentile life retained for a time a survival of Judaic culture.   But meanwhile it is to be remarked that Paul now, for the first time, displays an antagonism to that which was the main object of the Jew's religion—the flesh.   To the mind of every Jew the test of religious sanctity was the wholeness of the outer man ; it was precisely on this ground that Paul himself had uttered his first prayer in deprecation of his thorn.   But at the present stage of his experience, the element of Paul's former glory had become the element of his aversion.   He had conceived for the first time a disposition towards asceticism—a desire to be emancipated from the world *as* a world : it is nothing less than this that breathes in the aspiration, " Who shall deliver me from this body of death ? " His second prayer in deprecation of his thorn pro-

ceeded from exactly an opposite motive to that which
had dictated his first.   When first he " besought the
Lord that it might depart " from him, it was because
he was at that time resting under the Jewish conviction that the thorn was an interference with that
wholeness of the flesh which the Jew above all things
reverenced.   But now when for the second time he
beseeches the removal of his thorn, it is for precisely
the contrary reason.   It is because the flesh in every
form has become to him an object of aversion, and
because he looks upon his thorn as simply a manifestation of that flesh.   If he had any longer believed
it to be an interference with the carnal, he would at
this stage have reverenced it ; but he looked upon it
as itself simply a part and illustration of that great
principle of materialism which he had begun to regard as the enemy of the spirit, and from whose
dominion and influence he was panting to be free.

What, then, was Paul's refuge from this second
struggle ?   We have seen his refuge from the first
conflict.   We have seen how, under the shadow of
the Arabian mountains, his sense of missionary hope
was stimulated anew by considering how his very
disqualification must tend to magnify the power of
God.   Here was a conflict of a different kind, which
needed a different close.   The subject of Paul's
second struggle was not his inadequacy as a missionary, but his frailty as a man, and his frailty by
reason of that flesh which, in the view of the old

religion, had constituted his glory. The problem
was, how was Paul to get free from this flesh?—who
was to deliver him from its body of death? Was
there any hope of an emancipation?—any prospect,
in the nature of things, that a time would come in
which the fetters of the spirit would be struck off,
and the soul would dwell aloft in the region of its
own uninterrupted purity?

In the view of Paul there was such a prospect.
I have said that this present stage of his experience
grew out of his first reaction against Judaism; yet,
strangely enough, it was from Judaism itself that he
received his earliest solution of the problem. In
breaking away from the old religion, he did not
break from it instantaneously; in emancipating himself from its present surroundings, he found his immediate refuge in its Messianic hope. It is at this
stage that Paul enters upon that phase of religious
experience which a few years afterwards appears so
conspicuously in his Epistles to the Thessalonians,
and which constitutes the earliest epistolary land-
mark we possess of his spiritual development. We
have seen that he was first presented to Christianity
in its supramundane form. The Christ whom he
saw on the plains of Damascus was really the Christ
of the future,—Christianity emancipated from all
local conditions. It is not surprising that a man,
whose first vision of Christianity had been the vision
of its immortalising power, should have fixed his first

Christian hope upon the fact of immortality. Christ was to him not an earthly memory. He was unassociated to his mind with the record of any human experience; he knew Him only as in the future He was to be. Is it wonderful that to him the future should have contained all his hope? Is it wonderful that, in his inability to go back into the scenes of the human history, his aspirations should have pressed forward into scenes not yet historical, and should have revelled in the prospective joys of days that were still to come.

This, then, was Paul's second refuge from that thorn in the flesh which had become to him the representative of the flesh itself. The world was to him a scene of misery; but there was another world. He was living in a state of things which made the bearing of life itself a cross; but there was coming another state of things which would reverse all present conditions. The sufferings of the Messiah had been accepted in the room of the ancient sacrifices, and through their acceptance prosperity had been secured to mankind. But it never occurred to Paul at this stage of his experience that the benefits of the Christian sacrifice were to take effect here and now. It was to a future sphere that he looked for the glorious results of the reconciliation between God and man. This earth as it stood was to him incapable of reconciliation,—it wanted renewal through its whole centre and circumference. Noth-

ing but an abolition of the present system of things
could remedy the evils of the flesh, or make it a fit
tabernacle for the indwelling of the Divine Spirit.
The first coming must be supplemented by a second.
Paul, indeed, was not peculiar here; he held it in
common with all the disciples. But his peculiarity
lay in the fact that to him the second coming seemed,
in order of time, to have taken precedence of the
first. The Christ whom he saw at Damascus had
been rather the Christ of the return than the Christ
of the original advent; he had been born out of due
time, in the sense that he had been privileged to witness the earliest of those manifestations which his
contemporaries referred to the latter times. It is
not surprising, therefore, that his gaze should originally have fastened upon the second coming, almost
to the exclusion of the first. He was as yet in the
days of his spiritual youth, and he had that experience which is common to all youth—the tendency
to see the future at the door, and to behold it without perspective. To-morrow was in its impression
more vivid than to-day, and to the interests and
claims of to-morrow the mind and heart of the
apostle were absorbingly directed.

That such is the prevailing tone of Paul's mind
at this period will be apparent to any one who
studies carefully the spirit and tenor of his two
epistles to the Thessalonians. It would not represent the tenor of these epistles to say that they con-

tain many references to the second coming; they
are themselves essentially and exclusively epistles
of the second coming. They breathe and exhale the
atmosphere of a life that is to be. They are not,
indeed, speculative in tone, but purely practical;
yet their practical element itself is founded upon
grounds not of the present but of the future, and
the virtues which are most commended are those
which stretch into that future. The Thessalonian
converts are exhorted to an attitude of waiting.[1]
They are incited to a spirit of hope.[2] They are
enjoined to cultivate a spotless life, that they may
be pure in the sight of the second advent.[3] They
are commanded to put a restraint upon their sorrow
in the vision of the approaching joy.[4] They are
asked to maintain a watchful demeanour in the
light of the imminence of this revelation.[5] The
recompense they are required to look for is a recompense entirely beyond the present scene of things,
one which is only to be reaped when the present
scene shall have passed away.[6] So far from expect-
ing their harvest from the ripening and development
of the world in which they move, their greatest hope
of a harvest is to be found in the sense of that
world's moral retrogression and apostasy.[7] It is
not surprising that, as the sum and consummation

---

[1] 1 Thess. i. 10.   [2] 1 Thess. ii. 19.   [3] 1 Thess. iii. 13.
[4] 1 Thess. iv. 13 *et seq*.   [5] 1 Thess. v. 1 *et seq*.
[6] 2 Thess. i. 5-10.   [7] 2 Thess. ii. 1 *et seq*.

of the whole, the Christian virtue which shines as a
star in the kingdom of the Father is the virtue of
expectant endurance, and that, in predominance over
all other things, they are asked to cultivate the
" patience of Christ." [1]

Such, according to Paul at this stage of his history, was to be the first effect of the Christian sacrifice.   The sacrificial life and death of the Son of
man had taken the place of the Jewish offerings,
and had purchased, alike for Jew and Gentile, a
reconciliation to the favour of heaven.   But whereas
to the Jew the favour of heaven was manifested in
the things that are seen and temporal, it was by the
mind of Paul referred to the things that are not seen
and eternal.   It did not occur to him at this stage
of his experience to look for the fruits of Divine
reconciliation in an improvement and a development
in the constitution of the present world.   From the
constitution of the present world his mind had experienced a revolt.   There was a rupture between
his sympathies and the works and ways of men.   A
hard and fast line had been drawn between his conception of what actually was, and his conception of
what ought to be ; and it did not as yet enter into
his thoughts to conceive the possibility of a Divine
advent, whose professed object should be to restore
and renovate the existing fabric.   The existing fabric
was destined to pass away.   Every stage of its his-

[1] 2 Thess. iii. 5.

tory was to be a stage downwards, a step nearer to the completion of its process of dissolution. The scene of man's amelioration was to be a new heaven and a new earth. Physical nature and human nature had alike proved themselves inadequate to the restoration of the Divine image; in the destruction of physical nature, and in the transformation of human nature, could the restoration of that image alone be found.

The position here assumed by Paul is at first sight one of worldly pessimism. And yet, a deeper reflection will show us that in its essence it was not so. Looked at from his present attitude, Paul might be regarded as an ascetic, as a man whose only desire was to be emancipated from contact with material forms. And yet in reality nothing could be further from the fact; strictly speaking, the reverse was true. So far from wanting to be emancipated from material forms, Paul desired to enjoy with these forms a closer and a more blameless contact. However much he had broken with the doctrine of circumcision, he had far from broken with the secular hope of the Jewish nation. He had accepted Christ as the realisation of the Messianic idea, but he had accepted Him in His most Messianic and Judaic aspect. He saw in Him one who had purchased by a Divine sacrifice a future inheritance of temporal glory, whose fulness and completeness would compensate for the dearth and barrenness

of the present scene. It was no mystical inheritance on which his mind was now set. It was a
world such as his countrymen had loved to picture
—a world of thrones and principalities and powers,
in which the highest seats would be reserved for
the best men. It was a land which should realise
the dreams of patriarch and prophet—a land flow-
ing with milk and honey, abundant with the fruits
of plenty and of peace. It was a country which
should be the highway of the nations, the focus of
culture, the meeting-place for all the products of
human civilisation—a region in whose prosperity
the prosperity of the surrounding earth would be
secured. Paul's hope of the second advent was a
secular hope, and his reason for desiring it was his
attraction towards the secular. If he had despised
the flesh, if he had looked down upon materialism
in itself, he would have seen in its abasement no
ground for regret. It was because he did not despise the flesh, it was because he saw in the material
world the possibility of better things, that he desired the advent of these better things. It was
precisely because in principle he was no ascetic,
that he longed for the abolition of what he believed
to be the corruption of God's way upon the earth;
it was his hope for a new and a higher physical
world that prompted him to pray that the present
system of things might come to an end.

CHAPTER VII.

PAUL'S THIRD STRUGGLE AND ITS RESULT.

I HAVE said that when Paul speaks of having besought the Lord thrice for the removal of his thorn, he seems to me to indicate that the struggles of his spiritual life had divided themselves into three distinct and successive classes. The first class consisted of the conflicts of the missionary—the struggles of the prospective apostle of the Gentiles to overcome the barrier of his own humiliation. The second embraced the conflicts of the man—the wakening in the human heart of the sense of its own sin by reason of its very contact with a higher and a holier life. One other class still remained to complete the good fight in which the human spirit had to engage ere it could finish its course with joy. Hitherto its struggles had all been with itself; it was now to enter into battle with others. Its previous warfare had arisen from the contrast be-tween its own light and its own darkness; its remaining strife was to arise from beholding its actual light imputed to motives of darkness.

I have called the first struggle Arabian, because it took place under the shadows of Sinai. I have called the second Antiochian, because it found its initiative movement contemporaneously with the time when Antioch began to be the second centre of the Christian Church. I shall call the third Galatian, because it seems to have had its beginning and to have experienced its fiercest hour in connection with that Church of Galatia to which the apostle dictated one of his epistles.

It will be observed that these three struggles exhibit the progress of Paul's mind through three different spheres. The Arabian conflict brought him into contact with the contrast between himself and the Divine life. The Antiochian conflict brought him into contact with the contrast between the higher and the lower nature within himself. The Galatian conflict was to bring him into contact with the contrast between himself and others. In the first instance, his struggle arose from contemplating his own darkness in comparison with the light of God. In the second instance, it arose from contemplating the darkness of one part of his nature in comparison with another side which had been illuminated by the Divine Spirit. In the third instance, it was to arise from hearing the light which was in him itself called darkness, from being confronted with opposi-

tion and with obloquy, not in those respects in
which he was blameworthy, but precisely in those
aspects of his character wherein he had experienced
the renewing effects of grace.

This third conflict, then, came neither from God
nor from his own nature, but from the malice of his
contemporaries. It marked the earliest division in
the Christian camp, the first moment in which there
began to appear any difference of tendency among
the followers of the Cross. Hitherto the community
of Christians had refused to regard itself as a dissent
from the faith of Judaism. Judaism had looked
upon it as a dissent, but the Christian community
had taken a different view. The only difference
between the followers of Christ and the followers
of the ancient worship had up to this time been, that
the former had proclaimed the realisation of what
to the latter was still only a hope. In such a claim
there was no heresy. It was perfectly competent
for a Jew at any time to say that he recognised in
the world the presence of the looked-for Messiah.
The recognition might be a mere fancy, and in any
case it would be necessary to subject the statement
to the test of examination; but the statement in
itself was in no sense adverse to the spirit of
Judaism, and in no sense disqualified a man for
being a member of its communion. Accordingly, we
are not surprised that the first followers of Jesus did
not regard themselves as the less Jews because they

were Christians. It might even be said for them, and be claimed by them, that they were Jews in a peculiar sense,—that they were animated by a patriotic zeal to see the realisation of the national hope, and to hasten the advent of the national glory. Whatever opposition they encountered from the mass of their countrymen, it was originally an opposition in no sense connected with any charge of disloyalty to the faith of their fathers. They were opposed at first on grounds political rather than religious, and even while objects of secular suspicion, were allowed to retain their place in the membership of the Jewish synagogue.

But it was a very different matter when the Christian community began to modify the worship of the past. To say that the Messiah had come was not in itself a heresy; it was a thing to be determined by evidence. But to say that because the Messiah had come there was no longer any need for circumcision, was to strike at the very roots of the old religion. When the Christian community called in question the doctrine of circumcision, it turned the opposition against itself into a new channel. It was not possible any longer to regard it as a Jewish sect; it assumed the aspect of a separate religion. It was inevitable that it should be so. From a Jewish point of view, no one can wonder at the horror with which the movement against circumcision was received by those who still retained the desire to be ranked as members of the Church of Israel. The case may be paralleled by imagining a section within the Church of England who should profess to dispense with the sacrament of the Lord's Supper, on the ground that Christianity had opened the way to a more inward and a more mystical communion. The Church of England is vastly tolerant of different shades of religious belief within her own pale—more tolerant than any other Church in Christendom. But it is safe to say that, in such a case as this, there would not be one dissentient voice as to the judgment which ought to be pronounced; High, Low, and Broad Church alike would unite in demanding that the adherents of this new tenet should be forced to leave the fold. And why? Because this ceremony of communion involves something more than a doctrine. The doctrine which it involves might be had without it. But it constitutes, *itself*, the essential bond of church membership—the badge which distinguishes those inside from those outside the pale. So was it in even a more pronounced sense with the ceremony of circumcision. If the Lord's Supper is the badge of fellowship with the Church, circumcision was the badge of fellowship alike with the Church and with the State; it was that which distinguished the Jew both in religion and in politics from the inhabitants of all other lands. It had, no doubt, a doctrinal bearing; it symbolised the sacri-

ficial surrender of the soul to God. But it was not
its doctrine which made it indispensable; that could
have existed in its absence. It was the fact that
it constituted to the Jewish nation the ground of
its political and religious communion, which placed
the man who should violate it in the position of one
who had committed treason against his country.

That man was Paul. It was destined that he
should be the first to whom the task should be
committed of exposing the inadequacy of circumcision to constitute the life of a religious system.
It is not surprising that on Paul should have fallen
all the odium which such a task involved. His
opposition to the doctrine of circumcision was not
only the first step in the final rupture between
Christianity and Judaism, it was the initial movement in the rending of that robe of the Master
which had hitherto been seamless. It revealed for
the first time the discords which already lay latent
within the heart of Christendom. It separated the
army of the "Captain of salvation" into two great
camps, which, however closely they might join together against a common enemy in time of war,
were ever to be in mutual antagonism in the season
of outward peace. From the very beginning Paul
had recognised that he had a mission to the Gentiles,
but he did not recognise at the beginning that his
mission to the Gentiles was to lead through any
other than the old familiar way. Under the shadows

of Sinai he had begun to breathe a freer and a more salubrious atmosphere — the atmosphere of patriarchal times, but it was still the native air of Israel. He had realised the universality of that promise which had made Abraham the medium of blessing to all the families of the earth, but it had never occurred to him that this blessing should come through any other door than the old gate of circumcision. Now for the first time, he had burst the barriers of that gate, had become, in an absolute sense, the apostle of the Gentiles. He had recognised the truth not only that the Gentile should have the Gospel preached equally with the Jew, but that he should be allowed to receive the Gospel through his own natural channels. He might obtain the patriarchal privilege without subjection to the patriarchal conditions, might be reckoned a child of Abraham without undergoing the ceremony of circumcision.

The result was that Paul immediately became the mark for general obloquy throughout the theocratic community. Not only did Christianity pass into a more distinctive opposition to Judaism, but within the pale of Christianity itself there arose the internecine strife between a Judaic and a Gentile principle. Upon Paul, as the representative of the Gentile principle, the weight of the recrimination fell. That recrimination was bitter and deep, and its sting lay in the fact that it attacked the apostle

in what he believed to be his strong points. It was
on the ground of an apostolic call that he had
ventured to form and to follow an independent
personal opinion ; it was natural, above all things,
that the earliest assault should be made precisely
on this claim to apostleship.   Accordingly, the first
attack on Paul was directed against the very fact of
his mission.   He had claimed to have received a
call through as direct a communion with the Master
as had been enjoyed by the earliest disciples. Where
was the evidence for such communion ?   He had
based it upon a vision ; what proof was there that
the vision was a reality ?   It was not in vision that
the Master had appeared to *them*.   Their apostolic
call had been founded on a communion which had
manifested itself in an intercourse with the man
Christ Jesus, which had received the proof of its
reality from the sound of a human voice and the
touch of a living hand.   But here was a man who
professed to have obtained his mission from a voice
that had passed away from earth, to have been impelled by the touch of a hand that had vanished
from the human scene.   How could such a profession be substantiated ?   What evidence was there
that it was not a dream or a delusion, the offspring
of madness, or the creature of imagination ?   It was
the call to a new gospel, a gospel which cut at the
roots of all that had been cherished by ancient
Israel ; surely such a call must be supported by

irresistible and incontrovertible evidence—evidence resting upon a higher and a more impregnable ground than the uncorroborated visions of an individual soul.

From this doubt as to the accuracy of Paul's observation, the transition was easy to a disparagement of his character. Had his actual life been harmonious with his apostolic claim? had his conduct in the outward world tallied with his professed experience of an inward illumination? If it had not done so, there was no need of further argument; his mission was at once disproved and discredited. Accordingly, the next attack on Paul was directed not so much against his opinions as against his personality. Instead of examining the historical circumstances under which he professed to have received his vision, his Judaic adversaries confronted what appeared to them to be the imperfections of his apostolic character. No one can read the Epistle to the Galatians, and the two epistles to the Corinthians, without being impressed with the fact that the life of the apostle was being subjected to a severe and an unjust criticism. In three directions we find that his ministerial character is assailed. It is assailed in respect of its power; insinuations are ventilated that his letters express a more authoritative tone than is borne out by his actual presence. It is assailed in respect of its motives; suggestions are made that he is using his apostolic claim for the sake of obtaining a livelihood. It is assailed in respect of its consistency; assertions are spread abroad that he himself has not been uniform in his repudiation of the doctrine of circumcision, but that in practice he has veered about like the changes of the wind.

It is to meet these charges mainly that the epistles to Galatia and Corinth are written. It is in these that he claims the signs of an apostle, and appeals for corroboration to the testimony of his converts. It is in these that he asserts the unselfishness of his motives, and declares how, in the midst of ministerial work, he has laboured for his daily livelihood by the toil of his own hands. It is in these that he maintains the uniform consistency of his practice, and appeals in confirmation of that consistency to the persecutions he had never ceased to suffer. Reading between the lines of these epistles, we see a retrospective light cast back on the intermediate years between his letter to the Church of Galatia and his letter to the Church of Thessalonica. In his epistles to the Thessalonians there is as yet no note of internecine war. The only struggle which there manifests itself is the conflict between the soul and the present world—a conflict which drives the apostle to seek his hope in another and a future world. But here Paul's foes are those of his own household, and the attack directed against him is an attack not against his weakness but against the points in his life which were really strong.

We are led, therefore, to the conclusion that this third struggle in the spiritual experience of St Paul must have had its origin at a period subsequent to the writing of the epistles to the Thessalonians, and previous to the writing of those to the Galatians, Corinthians, and Romans. It ushers us, accordingly, into a new and distinct epoch of Paul's spiritual history. It is at this stage that, in my opinion, we are to seek for the third of those occasions in which, according to his own testimony, he besought the Lord for the removal of his thorn. For it must be evident, even on the most superficial view, that in this attack upon his apostolic pretensions, the sense of his physical defect must have returned to him with redoubled force and with intensified pain. He claimed to be possessor of apostolic power. Might not his enemies point to his thorn, and say, "Physician, heal thyself." If he had been given the power to cure others, why did he carry in his own body the marks of dilapidation and disease? The signs of an apostle were the possession of healing gifts, alike over body and mind. Was it reasonable to suppose that a man who possessed such gifts would himself be in a condition of corporeal weakness, would himself require the aid of those very bodily ministrations which it was his special prerogative to alleviate and remove ?   Was not the very fact of such bodily weakness a conclusive and irrefragable proof that Paul did not possess those powers which he professed to wield, and that the heavenly vision on which he based his apostolic claim had existed only in the dream of his own imagining ?

Such was, undoubtedly, the reasoning of Paul's enemies. It is not too much to say that never before had his thorn cost him such pain. Not even under the shadows of Arabia had it brought to him so much bitterness. Under the shadows of Arabia its sting consisted in awakening the memories of past evil ; here, for the first time, its sting was turned against that in Paul which was really good. His thorn was no longer an attack merely upon that which needed penalty and expiation, it was an attack on that which marked the growth of a new life. We have evidence from the second group of his epistles how keenly he had felt this sting. We have evidence that in this third and final struggle, there was revealed to Paul's own mind how much of the human element was still left within him. He had imagined that, by fixing his thoughts entirely upon a future world, and seeking to forget the present hour, he could emancipate himself from all earthly annoyances. That imagination was now proved to be a dream. The attack on Paul's character, the attack on that part of his character which he felt to have been purified, roused again all his interest in the passing hour. It showed him that the Thessalonian standpoint was as yet impossible. He could not find rest from the present by merely surrendering himself to a hope of the future; the present was a fact, the future was an idea, and the fact was stronger than the idea. Men recriminated him in the actual world; he could not keep down his indignation by simply telling himself that there was another world coming in the future. If there was to be a refuge from present evil, it could only be found in present good. To emancipate himself from earthly annoyances by simply cherishing the faith that the earth and all therein would by-and-by be burned up, was to comfort himself by a mere negation; it was to conquer his annoyances by suppressing the cause of them. There was clearly a higher state possible—to conquer them while their cause yet remained. Hitherto he had only cherished the hope of putting them down; the highest course was to rise above them without putting them down. That goal could not be reached by the Thessalonian method; he felt so now in his deepest experience. He might still cherish the hope of the advent of a better world, but that hope could not be the immediate source of his strength. The immediate source of his strength must be an immediate good, something which could be realised here and now. If he was to reach an asceticism which would lift him above the world's sting, he must reach it not by seeing in the dim future the coming of another world, but by an instantaneous translation into some higher and heavenly life.

It was while meditating on this theme that there came into the mind of Paul a new and a great thought — a thought which was to transform his whole spiritual experience, and to make him, in his own words, " a new creature." He had been anxious to prove that he possessed the signs of an apostle; but were the signs of an apostle the ultimate evidence of Christian power ? Were there not signs lying behind the apostolic ? Was not the ultimate evidence of Christian power the possession of higher marks than those which designated apostleship— the marks of the Lord Jesus ? And were not the marks of the Lord Jesus precisely those credentials which he, of all men, could reproduce ? His enemies slighted him because he was the possessor of a thorn ; but had not the Master a whole crown of thorns ? Was not the life of the Son of man essentially a life of sorrows ? was not His greatest miracle the power to bear these sorrows ? Why should this element have been altogether overlooked by those who laid claim to Christian apostleship ? Men seemed to think that the only miracles of the Divine life were miracles of action; did they not forget that the Divine life itself was a miracle of bearing ? If he, Paul, could succeed in reproducing that life, if he could succeed in repeating, in his own experience, the patience, the gentleness, and the resignation with which the Son of man bore His cross, would he not furnish by the very possession of his thorn a higher proof of apostleship than could ever be given to the world by the mere spectacle of its removal?

And here it was that there burst upon the mind of Paul a new prospect of emancipation from the troubles of earth. In the epistles to the Thessalonians his only solace had been the hope that there would come in the future, and perhaps in the near future, an advent of the Lord which would produce a change in earthly conditions. The hope now dawned upon him that this change might come not in the future but in the present, that, instead of needing to wait for it, he might at this very moment be translated into a new atmosphere, made the recipient of a higher life. He had been looking forward to the time when he should be caught up to meet the Lord in the air; might not his spirit be caught up now? Was the presence of the Master limited to an hour of death—either the death of the individual or the death of the world? Was there no possibility of being ushered into union with the life of Christ until the silver cord was loosed and the golden bowl was broken? Could the spirit of man not be translated into the upper air while yet it was environed in this tabernacle of clay? If the Son of man Himself had spoken

L

of dwelling in heaven even while He was yet on earth, might not His followers also be in heaven while yet they trod the earthly scene? In a word, might not a disciple of Jesus be lifted without death into close and immediate communion with the life of God, be translated in his higher nature into an existence separate from and above the world, and made a citizen of the heavenly state whilst yet in human form he inhabited the sphere of men?

Such was Paul's question. The answer to it was the close of his third great struggle, the response to his final petition that his thorn might depart from him. That answer was immediate. Paul seemed to find, in a moment, in the twinkling of an eye, the goal after which he had been striving for long and weary years. Even in the solitudes of Arabia he had found no permanent rest from his thorn. He had only rested there under a sense of the overwhelming power of God, under a conviction that God's power might be perfected through the very instrumentality of his physical weakness. But here he was able to take a higher flight, to reach a deeper rest. There had burst upon him the conviction that the Divine power of Christianity was itself simply the strength to sustain weakness, that the earthly glory of the Master had mainly consisted in His ability to support with unmurmuring love the weight of a bitter thorn. And the thought

entered into the mind of Paul that he, by the very
fact of his suffering, might be united to Christ.
The thought entered into his heart that the very
physical weakness which seemed to deny the truth
of his apostolic claim might become the vehicle
for lifting him into the immediate presence of the
Master. His cross was a reproach amongst men;
what if it should raise him into the life of God?
He felt that it had so raised him. He felt that,
instead of needing to wait for the advent of heaven
to earth, he himself had already made his advent
from earth into heaven. He had been translated
without seeing death. He had been borne aloft
into the third heaven. He had been carried up
into the very bosom of the Master and made to
lie upon His breast. He had been allowed to
anticipate the second advent, to enter here on
earth into the fellowship, the communion, the
citizenship of the life everlasting. And the gate
by which he had entered in was just the despised
gate of his own sufferings, just the avenue of his
thorn. The hand by which he had clasped the
Messiah was the pierced hand which made him
the byword of his contemporaries; the door by
which he had approached the presence of the
Divine life was precisely that battered, mutilated
door which in the view of his countrymen precluded him from any share in that presence. In
a deeper sense than ever before, God had now

said to his soul, "My strength is made perfect in your weakness."

Here, then, is a new stage of Paul's spiritual experience. He is no longer merely waiting for Christ's second advent; he has gone himself to meet it. He is no longer solacing himself with the thought that a time is coming when he shall be lifted above the present world; he is solaced with the conviction that he has been lifted above the present world already. The epoch through which we are passing in St Paul's spiritual history is that period extending from the writing of the epistles to the Thessalonians to the writing of the letter to the converts of the world's metropolis. The materials for estimating its character will be found in the epistles to the Galatians, Corinthians, and Romans. The attitude of Paul in all these writings is the attitude of a man who has emancipated himself from the cares of the present world by a process of spiritual asceticism; so far, the letters to the Galatians, Corinthians, and Romans are in harmony with those to the Thessalonians. But the difference lies here: the asceticism in the epistles to the Thessalonians is the asceticism of a man who looks forward to a coming heaven; that of the four later epistles is the asceticism of a man who believes himself to have already entered into heaven and to have left the present world actually behind. That this

is the character of these later letters it would
not be difficult to prove. It would be very easy
to draw up from each of them a catalogue of
passages corroborative of the assertion that Paul's
attitude to mundane things is that of one who
looks down upon a surmounted standpoint. I
shall, indeed, hereafter show that in the latest
of the letters — that to the Romans — there are
already discernible the traces of a further transition, the foreshadowings of a subsequent stage of
development. Nevertheless, the general tone of
these four epistles is the same, and, as I have
said, nothing could be easier than to prove it
by quotations. I think, however, that in this
instance there is a more excellent way. I believe the best method will be to take up the
points in these epistles in which the spiritual
nature of Paul exhibits a development from his
previous standpoint, and to consider in what respect his attitude towards current opinion has
undergone a change of posture. It will be found
that in no case has his later stage denied or
falsified the old. It will be found that the new
culture has exhibited itself not in the way of
negation but by the process of supplement, not
by destroying the ancient landmarks but by filling up that which is behind. No doubt, when
we fill up that which is behind, we have altered
the aspect of all our former view; the discovery

of one hidden feature of a landscape may transform to our mind the whole scene.   None the
less does it remain true that the transformation
has been effected not by elimination but by increase, not by pulling down but by building up.
To a more detailed consideration of this subject
we shall revert in the next chapter.

CHAPTER VIII.

DEVELOPMENT OF PAUL'S RELIGIOUS VIEWS.

THERE is a strong analogy between the physical and the spiritual nature of man. No change can take place in any part of an outward organism without producing a change in every part of that organism. Even so is it in the world of mind. The entrance of a single new idea might be thought to be a very small thing. In reality, however, it is impossible that any single idea can enter the mind without producing a change in every department of thought. The casting of a stone into the water is in itself a merely local occurrence, but its effect is unlimited; it sets in motion circles without end. Even so, the birth of a thought has issues far beyond itself; it wakens eddies which stir all the depths of the spirit and pulsate through every pore of the man's mental being.

We have seen that in the mind of Paul there was born a new thought. We have seen that his third spiritual struggle had been closed by his awakening to the conviction that he himself had already passed beyond the reach of his earthly cares. He had come to learn something of the luxuries of death without its pains. He had been lifted on this side the grave into an atmosphere above the earth, from which he looked down upon his former self and saw all things changed. It was impossible, indeed, that such a change in his own standpoint could take place without modifying his view of the whole past. How radical was the transformation he himself declares by describing himself as a new creature to whom old things had passed away. Nevertheless, as we have said, the change in Paul's view is not to be looked for in the direction of revolution. It was not a development by revolt but by supplement. Things were made new to him not by a destruction of the past, but by a vision of the past from the height of a higher hill. The landscape wears a different aspect from different positions. Paul had reached a radically new position, and his landscape was renewed. The old forms were there, the old substances were there, the old groupings were there ; but there was a light playing upon them which did not play before, and the effect of that light was to make all things new.

Let us now go on to see in what respects this new light was likely to modify, and actually did modify, Paul's previous system of thought. What was likely to be the first direction in which the change in Paul's

mental attitude should begin to manifest its effect?
Clearly, its earliest influence would be exhibited in
supplementing his view of the doctrine of resurrection. I do not say that in every case such would
have been the first result, but in Paul's case it not
only was so but could not have been otherwise. We
have already indicated that Paul was pre-eminently
and essentially the apostle of the resurrection. He
was distinguished from all the other primitive disciples in this, that he alone came to the knowledge
of Christ after the visible form of Christ had passed
away. His earliest association with the Master had
been the association with one who had triumphed
over death. He had not even been drawn to Him
by any human traditions of His earthly life and
ministry : these all came to him subsequently. His
first sight had been the sight of the unearthly Christ,
of the Christ who had been great in spite of earth.
It is not surprising, therefore, that the earliest note
of Paul's gospel should have been the note of resurrection. That it was the earliest note of his gospel
is abundantly evident from his epistles to the Thessalonians, where from beginning to end the mind of
the reader is made to centre on the hope of the coming Lord and the accompanying transformation of
all things. But the point for us to observe is the
fact that in the epistles to the Thessalonians this is
still only a hope. The resurrection from death, the
abolition of the old system, the translation of the

soul into a higher life, is as yet with Paul merely something which is to come, an event which is to be consummated at the end of the days. But with the close of what I have called the Galatian struggle there comes a change of thought. At the close of that struggle we have found Paul permeated by a new consciousness—the sense of being actually and at this moment in union with Christ. The effect of such a consciousness upon the old belief in resurrection was inevitable. It was not destructive but reconstructive; it brought the idea from the future into the present. The resurrection from the dead ceased to be regarded as a mere event; it came to be viewed as a process—a process whose consummation was, indeed, in other worlds, but whose beginning and development were here. If Paul had already been translated into the life of Christ, if his own consciousness told him that he had passed even now beyond the bounds of death, was it not clear that henceforth the idea of resurrection must itself change its aspect, that the rising from the dead must hereafter be regarded, not as a mere catastrophe taking place at the end of all things, but as a process of upward development, whose beginnings are in the world below and whose consummation alone is in the world above?

And this view of the subject clearly appears in that remarkable passage of St Paul's epistles which, more than any other, represents his doctrine of re-

surrection—the fifteenth chapter of 1st Corinthians.
Let us look for a moment at that verse, which is the
nucleus of the whole passage, " So also is the resurrection of the dead. It is sown in corruption; it is
raised in incorruption : it is sown in dishonour; it
is raised in glory: it is sown in weakness; it is
raised in power: it is sown a natural body; it is
raised a spiritual body." [1]   There are two questions
which arise in connection with these words,—What
is that which is sown ? and What is the nature of the
sowing ?   To each of these we would briefly advert.

And first, when Paul says, " It is sown in corruption; it is raised in incorruption :" of what is he
speaking ?   What is the " it " ?   Most people will
answer spontaneously, " The human body, of course."
And yet, the context of the passage does not grammatically bear out this view. The subject of the
sentence is not the body but the resurrection itself,
" so is the resurrection of the dead." Paul is not
speaking of the gradations through which the *body*
passes, but of the gradations through which the
resurrection passes. He wants to emphasise his belief that the resurrection is itself a process in which
the incipient stage is sowing and the final stage
reaping, in which the beginning is weakness and the
consummation power, in which the opening scenes
are in dishonour and the ultimate sights in glory.
This is unmistakably his meaning, and it is in strict

[1] 1 Cor. xv. 42-44.

harmony with the whole previous context. In that context he has been labouring to show that the quickening of the seed is, even in physical nature, not an act but a process. A necessary part of the seed's development is that stage of dishonour which marks its incorporation with the soil. Its resurrection begins, not with that morning in which it appears in fruit or flower, but with the day in which it is laid beneath the ground : its burial is the first step in its rising. Paul says that in this respect the resurrection of the human spirit bears a striking analogy to that of the physical seed. To the human spirit, as to the physical seed, there comes a time of fruit and flower, a morning in which old things have passed away and all things are made new. But with the spirit, as with the seed, this is not the beginning but the end of resurrection. Here, too, we behold, not a sudden catastrophe, but only the last stage of a great process of development whose earliest stage was underground. The spirit, like the seed, had to climb a ladder of resurrection—a ladder whose summit, indeed, was in the heavens, but whose base was planted underneath the earth. The birth of the risen life was not in the world above but in the world below.

It may be asked why we should speak of the first stage of resurrection as a stage of the human *spirit ;* why not regard it as having found its inauguration in the planting of the body within the ground ? The

answer to this question is really the answer to the
second of those inquiries involved in this passage of
St Paul. If the first question is, "What is that
which is sown?" the second is, "What is the nature
of the sowing?" The popular view is, that when
Paul says, "it is sown in corruption," he is speaking
of the process of burial, is alluding to the humiliation of that moment in which the once vigorous
human body is sent to mingle with the dust. A
little reflection will convince us that this is not
Paul's meaning. We in modern times are so familiar with the disposal of the dead by interment, that
we forget how comparatively rare was this practice
in the ancient world. We forget that cremation,
and not burial, was the mode of sepulture most
widely prevalent in the thought of those lands outside of Judea. We must remember that the epistle
in which the reference occurs was written to the
Church of Corinth—a city in the very heart of Gentiles, and permeated by Gentile associations. Is it
conceivable that, when Paul wished to describe to
them the humiliating nature of that first stage in
which resurrection had its birth, he should have
adopted a metaphor which, however familiar to the
modern ear, was to those to whom he was speaking
an association of ideas unknown in fact?

We conclude, then, that when Paul speaks of the
seed being sown in corruption, he is not alluding to
the modern practice of interring the body in the

ground.   He is not, in fact, alluding to the body at
all.   He is speaking of the principle of Divine life.
He is trying to emphasise his belief that the life of
Christ in the soul has its beginnings in great humility.   He means to say that this life, instead of waiting for the purification of the natural man, descends
into the natural man in his present unpurified condition.   It does not tarry until the house has been
emptied, swept, and garnished; it comes down into
the house while it is yet full of corruption, uncleansed,
unbeautified.   It comes as the light comes into the
physical world.   It rises in a special corner of the
soul while all other corners are as yet in night.   The
hour in which the Divine life first enters into the
heart of man is precisely that hour in which the
heart of man is in its deepest and darkest gloom.
The seed which is sown in it is doubtless a principle
of vitality, but it is a principle of vitality which has
emptied itself into humiliation, which has conde-
scended to dwell amid conditions that are foreign
to its own nature and natural barriers to its own
development.   It has done in the soul what the Son
of man did in the world,—poured out its native
glory and assumed a servant's form.

Such is here Paul's view of that great process of
resurrection which was at one time regarded by him
as a mere sudden catastrophe taking place at the
end of all things.   What led him to change his
thought was his consciousness of a change in himself

He felt that there had come into him a new life—
that very life of which he had been dreaming in his
epistles to the Thessalonians. He felt that it had
come to him without waiting for his purification,
that it had descended upon him while yet he was
encompassed by the frailty of the flesh, that it had
been sown in corruption, in weakness, in dishonour.
And because he felt this in himself, he felt it to be
a possibility for all men. The resurrection from the
dead ceased any more to be to him a mere final
catastrophe; it became a part of human life itself.
It came to be regarded as a great process of development—a process which has its beginnings amid the
miry clay of earth, and which finds its initial movement amid the things which are seen and temporal.
It was by him to be looked upon henceforth not as
something whose coming would follow the dissolution of body and soul, but as a life whose advent
would begin while the soul was yet in the body, and
which would enable a man, even in the presence of
worldly forms, to feel that he had passed already
" from death unto life."

I come now to the second of those phases of
thought in which Paul's new experience exercised a
modifying influence upon his former opinions. If
the first and immediate change was that produced
upon his view of resurrection, the second was that
effected upon his view of revelation. It would perhaps be more correct to say that Paul's sense of

personal elevation into the Divine life for the first time developed the *idea* of revelation. The first idea of every religion is not that of revelation but of inspiration. When the question first occurred to the mind of man, "How can God commune with the human soul?" the answer which immediately suggested itself was that of a communication from without. Some thought of God as speaking audibly in the thunder-cloud and in the other voices of nature. Some thought of Him as sending messages to the soul through the ministry of angels. Some conceived Him as making His will known by a dream or a vision. Some figured Him as creating within the heart a state of ecstatic rhapsody which, for the time, made the man cease to be human, and caused him to become a mere passive organ of the Divine will. This last form is the idea of inspiration proper, and constitutes the earliest mode of prophetic illumination. The man is lifted out of himself, raised beyond his own consciousness, and deprived of his individual personality. He is made, for the time being, a breath of the Infinite Mind, and is compelled to become the recipient of a message which he does not understand.

But this inspiration is the opposite of revelation. It is distinctly different from a communication between the Divine and the human; it is the sublimation of the human into the Divine. It is really an erasure of the individual life of the creature. It is not a mode whereby the thoughts of God are made

the thoughts of man; it is a device by which the
thoughts of man are annulled and God becomes all
in all. Revelation is precisely the reverse of this.
Instead of being a depression, it is an elevation of
the human. Instead of being an annihilation of the
creature to make room for the Creator, it is a lifting
up of the creature to a spiritual level with the
Creator. However startling the assertion may sound,
it is literally true. No mind can reveal itself to
another mind unless they meet on a common bridge.
The point in which you reveal yourself to me is not
the point in which you are my superior, but the
point in which you are my equal. It is through a
community of experience that I receive the revelation. It is precisely because I have found a spot in
which my mind is not different from yours, precisely
because I have experienced a feeling which corre-
sponds and responds to the feeling of your heart,
that I am able to recognise in your words a revelation to my soul.

Now, I have said that to Paul belongs the pre-
eminence of having first passed over the boundary-
line that divides inspiration from revelation. In
him for the first time we find a disparagement of
supernatural gifts in comparison with habitual atti-
tudes of mind. Very strikingly is this evinced in
the thirteenth chapter of 1st Corinthians. He here
declares, in language which to his contemporaries
must have appeared very bold, that though he could

M

speak with the tongues of angels, though he had
faith that could remove mountains, though he had
knowledge that could understand all mysteries, it
would profit him nothing without the possession of
love. He declares that love is distinguished from
the other gifts of God precisely by the fact that
it is not supernatural, that it is something which
"abideth." The possession of prophetic powers, the
possession of mystical knowledge, the possession of
supernatural tongues, is but a transitory thing, and
it is transitory precisely because it is a state of
ecstasy in which the man is lifted out of himself and
made a passive organ; the moment he returns to
his humanity he loses his inspiration. But love is
a state of permanent equality between the man and
his object. It is a condition which can only exist
where there exists already a bridge of connection
between two minds. It is founded upon the possession of a common quality. It is built upon the
fact that one being is already in sympathy with
another. No being can be in sympathy with
another unless on the ground of equality: they can
only meet in love where they have already met in
nature. And therefore it is that in one of his later
epistles Paul insists on a community of nature as
a preliminary condition to any revelation between
God and man. He says that the love of God is
beyond the knowledge of every man who has not
himself already been " rooted and grounded in love,"

that it is only by the possession of this kindred mental state that one is able to comprehend the Divine nature in its fulness.[1] The thought is very close to the standpoint of the fourth Gospel. Paul, like John, sees in love the very nature of God—the length and the breadth, the height and the depth of His being. Like John also he sees that, to comprehend this love, a man must himself be loving, that, to catch a beatific vision of the Divine life, he must already be partaker in his own heart of that which constitutes the essence of Divinity. The latest utterance of the Christian consciousness is here but a re-echo of the Gospel's initial word, "Blessed are the pure in heart: for they shall see God."

And this explains the meaning of one of the most remarkable passages in Paul's epistles—the second chapter of 1st Corinthians. The idea of that chapter clearly is that a man can only understand God by being already recipient of the life of God. The thought is strikingly brought out in verse 11, "For what man knoweth the things of a man, save the spirit of man which is in him? even so the things of God knoweth no man, but the Spirit of God." What Paul says is this: In the human world none but a man can know a man. A dog cannot know a man; it can see, and even imitate his outward actions, but it cannot know himself. Even so, in the

[1] Eph. iii. 17-19.

spiritual world none but God can know God. The recognition of the Divine demands the possession of Divinity, or, which is the same thing, necessitates a participation in the Spirit of God. In order to understand a description of any earthly object it is necessary that the object in some form should have already passed through our experience; the eye must have seen it, or the ear must have heard it, or the heart must have conceived it. If the object has been foreign to the soul, it can never be revealed to the soul until a faculty has been created whereby it can be imagined. So is it with the spiritual world. Originally, it is foreign to the natural mind; eye has not seen it, ear has not heard it, and therefore the imagination cannot reproduce it—heart has not conceived it. Its nature is love, and love is unintelligible to the loveless. No words can make it intelligible; you can print it in four letters, but to print it is not to reveal it. You can only reveal it by imparting it. If you would communicate to any heart a revelation of the love of the Father, you must first create within that heart the idea of fatherhood and the sense of a father's love, must first inspire the soul to whom you speak with a spirit kindred to the message which you bring, and render luminous the narrative of Divine affection by implanting in the heart the feeling of human tenderness.

I pass now to the third of those doctrines which

received a fresh development from Paul's new standpoint; I mean his view of that relation in which
Christ stands to the human soul. The starting-
point of this inquiry is the fifth chapter of Romans.
The key-note of that chapter is struck in two words,
"much more." It is a key-note of conscious progress. Paul distinctly implies that at the time
when he was writing that epistle he was quite
aware of having taken a step in upward development. He says, in verse 10, "For if, when we
were enemies, we were reconciled to God by the
death of His Son, much more, being reconciled, we
shall be saved by His life." Can any one fail to
perceive that Paul is here recording an autobiographical experience, that he is describing precisely
those phases of the spiritual life through which he
himself is conscious of having passed? Can any
one fail to see that he is drawing a contrast between the height which he had then and there
attained, and the valley which he had inhabited in
the days of old? He tells us that there was a time
in which Christ was to him simply a reconciler, a
time in which he valued Christianity only as a
source of peace to the conscience that had outraged
God. He goes back in thought to the days of the
Arabian desert, when he stood under the shadow of
Sinai, and felt, for the first time, the sense of his
own unworthiness. He remembers how, under that
shadow, there had come to him a comfort in the

thought that the justification of man in the sight
of God had always lain in God's sight of a coming
sacrifice, had always consisted in the Divine vision
of a perfect offering yet to be. He remembers how,
at that time, the beauty of the Christ derived to him
its power from the fact that it stood between himself
and the blaze of the Divine purity, that it interposed
a mediating veil between his own miserable rags and
the spotless vesture of the Eternal. But now Paul
had transcended that position. He had not, indeed,
contradicted it; it was still as true to him as ever.
But it was no longer the whole truth. Christ was
still his reconciler, but He was something more;
He had become his second self. It was no longer
enough for Paul that a daysman should stand between himself and the majesty of the heavenly
Father; he must himself be united to that daysman. He had reached a point of the hill in which
he had ceased to look up to the sunbeam; the
sunbeam had flooded him with its own light. He
had once been saved by Christ's work; he was now
saved by His life. He had once beheld the image
of Christ in the heavens; he had now entered within those heavens. The spirit of Christ had become
his own spirit, the life of Christ his own life. He
was no longer a beholder; he was a recipient. He
was no longer a man contemplating his deliverance from bondage; he was a man who had forgotten the memory of his former chains in the

glad air of a liberty wherewith Christ had made him free.

If now we turn to another passage of this same epistle, we shall find confirmatory evidence that Paul was conscious of a changed relationship between himself and the Master. In Romans viii. 29, 30, he says,—"For whom he did foreknow, he also did predestinate to be conformed to the image of his Son; moreover whom he did predestinate, them he also called: and whom he called, them he also justified: and whom he justified, them he also glorified." Who can fail here again to recognise the notes of Paul's own biography, the record of his own spiritual experience? He is quite conscious in looking back that he has passed through four distinct stages—predestination, calling, justification, and glorification. And the reader is quite conscious with him that these had hitherto been precisely the stages in which his life had approximated to Christ. In looking back on the course of his spiritual history we see that he had drawn near to the Master just in these four degrees. We see him, according to his own testimony, experiencing at the hour of birth that act of Divine predestination which set him apart for the cause of Jesus, "God separated me from my mother's womb." We see him next receiving the call to a ministry, arrested by an act of Divine grace, and compelled against his will to fulfil the destiny of his birth. We see him then under the

shadows of Sinai, alone with the contemplation of
his past, and solitary in the prospect of his future;
yet even amidst his pain recognising the comfort of
the truth that his past could be atoned by a perfect
righteousness, and his future vindicated by a perfecting life; the age of predestination and the age of
calling has been succeeded by the age of justifying.
But even yet the development is not complete; he
has not yet reached the goal of his predestination—
the conformity to the image of Christ. That goal
came with the fourth and final stage—glorification.
It is the word we habitually use to describe the state
of the blessed dead; we speak of such as entering
into glory. Paul in a physical sense was not dead,
yet he is not afraid to appropriate even on earth the
condition of the saints departed. He is not afraid to
say that without passing through the valley of the
shadow he has entered already into the promised
land, has become partaker already of that beatific
glory which belongs to the life of those that have
fought a good fight and finished their course. He
has passed without dying from the Church militant
into the Church triumphant, and has exchanged the
sense of justification by Christ's blood for the deeper
sense of renovation by Christ's life.

And what is this sense of renovation by Christ's
life? It is simply that to which Paul had declared
himself predestinated from the beginning—conformity to the Master's image. The goal to which he

had been travelling had all along been this goal. I do not say he had all along recognised it; I believe he had not. It is one thing to see the course through which you have come when you have gained the top of a hill; it is another thing to trace that course when you are walking amid the encumbering shadow of the trees. In the period immediately subsequent to his Arabian experience Paul was walking under the shadow of the trees, and the prospect of the hill-top was hidden. There was present to him as yet only a sense of his own nothingness, and Christ was realised by him simply as the perfect righteousness that stood between himself and the majesty of heaven. Let us suppose that at this stage it had been told to Paul that a time was coming when he should utter these words, "We, with open face beholding as in a glass the glory of the Lord, are changed into the same image from glory to glory," what would have been his impression? He would have said, 'God forbid that I should utter such blasphemy.' He would have repudiated with horror and indignation the thought that he, a poor sinner, who owed everything he possessed to an act of Divine clemency, should aspire to be himself on terms of equality with that Divinity which had pardoned him. It would have seemed the wildest, the most daring presumption, that a creature which only yesterday had been dragged from the pit and from the miry clay, should immediately and instantaneously lift his head to claim fellowship with God Himself; if such a thought had entered his mind, he would have rent his clothes and implored forgiveness. But now from the top of the hill all was changed. He perceived that all along he had been travelling towards an unseen goal, a goal larger and deeper than his most aspiring dreams. He perceived that the object for which he was destined had been nothing less than a participation in the Divine image, nothing less than conformity to the very nature of God. In former days he would have deemed the dream of such a destiny blasphemous; it had now become essential to his very existence. It was no longer enough for him to be a Christian; he must be a sharer in the life of Christ, a partaker of His image, a member of His body. It was no longer enough for him to be reconciled through Christ's sacrificial blood; he must himself be inoculated with that blood, must himself be sent forth to fulfil the ministry of reconciliation. He must become the glory which he had gazed upon, must grow into the brightness on which his eyes had rested.

And this I take to be the time in which Paul made a remarkable discovery in the field of his spiritual experience. He found that all this time he had been unconsciously repeating that very form of suffering through which the Son of man had passed. The discovery is announced in a passage which we have already quoted by anticipation, but whose full light can only be seen from the summit of Paul's experience; I mean those words which he writes to the Church of Galatia, "God forbid that I should glory save in the cross of the Lord Jesus Christ, by whom the world is crucified unto me, and I unto the world." He declares in these words that his own personal sorrow has followed exactly the order of that road which the Master had pursued in ascending the Dolorous Way. His own experience had been that of a double crucifixion; the world had first been crucified to him, and then he had been crucified to the world. His first feeling had been that of simple pain, simple privation, simple resignation. The light of the world had gone out from him, and had left him mute and cold. He was dumb, indeed, under the mighty hand of God; he had murmured not at the dispensation. But there is a vast difference between the dumbness of submission and the song of acquiescence, and all the vastness of that difference had not as yet been felt by him; it was only an outward crucifixion. But now the crucifixion itself had been crucified; the muteness had passed into song. His spirit had accepted the thorn—accepted it not as a necessity but as a privilege. He had ceased to receive his calamity merely as a mandate of the Divine Will, beneath which he was bound to bow; he had come to welcome it as itself a gift of God. The world was not given back to him, but he

was made independent of its restoration. He
had ceased to value or to regret that which was
once a necessity of his life; he was "crucified to
the world."

Now it was in this twofold experience that Paul
discovered the striking analogy between his own
cross and the cross of Christ. His mind immediately reverted to the scene in the garden of Gethsemane. He remembered how, on that occasion, the
Master too had experienced a double crucifixion.
He, like His disciple, had besought the Lord three
times.[1] His first prayer was for the removal of His
thorn, "If it be possible, let this cup pass from me."
He had cherished a hope that He would be permitted to remain in the world until He should have
witnessed the visible establishment of His kingdom.
That hope had been dashed by the current of events.
The world was passing away from before His eyes,
and the figure of death stood in the breach. It was
a moment of outward crucifixion, and He felt it,
sorrowed over it, prayed against it. Then came the
two succeeding prayers, intermediate between the
weakness and the strength—the prayers in which
the Son of man had asked exemption not from His
thorn but from His desire to be rid of it, "If this
cup may not pass from me, except I drink it, Thy
will be done." And then, as a result of this latest
prayer, the strength had come. The Son of man

[1] Matt. xxvi. 39-44.

had risen erect in the scene of His former sorrow, and had confronted the spectacle of death without a pain. He had accepted His cup as a gift from the Father, had accepted it as itself a step in the development of His kingdom. The thorn had not been removed, but He had ceased to desire its removal. The gate of death had not been shut, but He had determined to make it the opening into a wider life; the world had been crucified to Him, but He was now crucified to the world.

Such in my opinion was the striking analogy which led Paul to the conclusion that he had been made conformable to the image of the Master, which led him to see in his own cross a repetition of that form of suffering which had constituted the cross of his Lord. The impression derived from this analogy never forsook him; it remained with him steadfast to the end. Whatever subsequent developments he was called to pass through, he never outgrew nor superseded the vividness of this experience: the future might broaden it, but it could not deepen it; it was already full. Hence through all his subsequent epistles there runs one common refrain — " Crucified together with Christ, I live; yet not I, for Christ liveth in me." From the day when he penned his letter to the Galatians until the day when he finished his course in the Roman capital, there appears, under endless variations, the one perpetual strain—the conviction of membership in a Divine body, and the confidence of fellowship with the sufferings of the Lord.

But Paul could not go so far without going further; the change in his relation to Christ's person involved a change in his relation to Christ's work. What was that work? Why was the Son of man called to experience this double process in the bearing of the cross? Paul answers, "He hath made Him to be sin for us, who knew no sin; that we might be made the righteousness of God in Him." [1] The idea evidently is that, in order to be the reconciler of fallen humanity, the Son of man had to put Himself in the place of fallen humanity. Before He could forgive, before He could atone, it was necessary that He should clothe Himself in the likeness of that which was naturally adverse to Him.[2] It was necessary that He should environ Himself with the circumstances, with the weaknesses, with the difficulties, of those who stood in His way, that He should try to see with their eyes, and, in a measure, to feel with their hearts. He must, in short, become the substitute for humanity, must put Himself in sympathy, even before He put Himself in fact, into the position of those who had violated the Father's law, and must impute to Himself by an act of Divine imagination the frailty of those lives which had thus been tempted to transgress.

Such was the work of Christ as Paul conceived it.

[1] 2 Cor. v. 21.   [2] Rom. viii. 3.

In all this there was to him nothing new. Even before he became a Christian he must have gathered from the later Isaiah that the Messiah, when He came, would be one who should bear the sins and carry the sorrows of His people, one on whom the Lord should lay the iniquities of us all. But the newness of Paul's present thought consisted not in his knowledge of the fact, but in his mode of applying it to his own practical experience. In the days of old, in the days when he had just emerged from the Arabian solitudes, and recovered from the first overpowering sense of the stern heights of Sinai, his comfort had lain in the reflection that, since Christ had reconciled the world, he too was reconciled. But now such a thought was no longer sufficient for him; it was still true, but it had ceased to be adequate. It was no longer enough for Paul that he should be reconciled; he must be a reconciler. It was no longer a sufficient consolation that he had ceased to stand in a relation of enmity to God; he must himself become partaker of that work by which this enmity had been superseded. Had he not been made conformable to Christ's image? Had he not received the indwelling of the very life and soul which dwelt in the Son of man? For what had he received it? not surely that he might be a mere passive recipient. Did not the conformity to the Divine image demand a conformity to the Divine life? If he had received the impress of Christ's person, was it not that he might repeat the form of Christ's work? Must not he too, like his Master, begin by putting himself in the place of others, and begin by doing so in thought before he did it in fact? Must not he too, by an act of Divine imagination, empty himself into the circumstances of fallen humanity, and endeavour to realise in his experience the frailties and the difficulties of erring souls? He had freely received; must he not now freely give? He had himself been reconciled; was it not henceforth his province and his duty to take up for others the ministry of reconciliation? [1]

That this experience in the heart of Paul came to him not at the very beginning but by a process of after development, is to my mind borne out by the fact that the later tone of his writings is much more mild than the earlier. If we take this middle group of his epistles, and consider that to the Galatians as standing at the beginning, and that to the Romans at the close, we shall be struck with the comparative mellowness of the latter fruit. The epistle to the Galatians is like the primrose after winter. It rises with fresh life—life prophetic of a warmer day, yet it is itself still struggling with the cold, and still impeded by the survivals of a more primitive culture. It is an epistle of storms, wherein the mind of the apostle reveals at every turn that it is in the presence of its enemies, and betrays in

[1] 2 Cor. v. 18.

every expression how little it has yet learned to bear.
But it may be said that this is the last blast of Paul's
winter; every after-stage of the day is increasingly
mild. Even ere the epistle closes, we have a hint
of warmer weather, "Henceforth let no man trouble
me, for I bear in my body the marks of the Lord
Jesus." The words indicate that the mind of Paul
is already conscious of getting beyond its trouble,
already awakening to the sense that the worst is
over. What is it that mitigates his pain? It is the
gradual dawning of the knowledge that he has a
higher ordination than the laying on of visible hands,
that the marks of Christ's own hand have been im-
printed on his frame. He feels that he has become
partaker of Christ's own nature, and that, being
partaker of His nature, it is too late in the day to
disturb himself as to whether he has received a genuine visible ordination. He feels something more
than that. If he is partaker of Christ's nature, is
he not thereby precluded from asserting himself
thus violently against the follies of his weak brother?
Does not the possession of Christ's image demand
the participation in Christ's work, and does not that
work consist in bearing the sins and weaknesses of
those who are still in the valley? Is it not incumbent on him, as one who has received the spirit of
the Master, to put himself in the place of those who
occupy an opposite standpoint from his own, to throw
himself into sympathy with their difficulties, and

N

seek to reproduce in his experience that very view
of the controversy which has set them in the meantime in antagonism to his work and teaching?

And when we come to the epistle to the Romans,
we find that Paul has already put in practice this
new vision of the crucified Christ. In his letter to
the Galatians, he had written amid storm and stress,
amid the sense of injured honour, and the contempt
of a mind which had come to look down upon the
mean and beggarly elements of former days. But
when he took up his pen to write to the Church
of the great metropolis, it would almost seem as
if the reconciliatory spirit of that metropolis had
already affected his soul. It would almost seem as
if, in the presence of that vast capital which had
gathered together the various types of man as a hen
gathereth her chickens under her wings, the individual differences between him and his adversaries
were lost and overshadowed in the perception of a
mightier underlying unity, in the vision of a bond of
humanity which made all men one. Be this as it
may, it is certain that in this epistle to the Romans
the mind of the apostle has overleapt its earlier
bitterness, has passed beyond that middle wall of
partition which in days of yore divided him from
Judaic Christianity. He had begun under the
shadows of Mount Sinai, and then he had revolted
from these shadows; he now goes back to incorporate the shadows with the sunlight. It is not

that he has ceased to recognise the existence of a middle wall; it is present to his eye as clearly and as opposingly as ever. What he does recognise is something above the wall, beneath the wall, and running through the wall. What is that something? Is it the vision of Christ's atoning work? In one sense, that had been known to Paul from the beginning,—known to him even while he remained in the faith of his fathers. The knowledge of that fact had not been sufficient to free him from polemical bitterness, nor to prevent him from applying to his adversaries his scourge of small cords. But what lifted Paul out of his bitterness was the knowledge of an additional fact which had only recently burst upon his view. It was the vision of the truth that, if he were a follower of Christ, he must himself be a sharer in Christ's atoning work. It was not enough to be reconciled; he must be a reconciler. And what did this mean? Was it anything less than the identification of himself with his adversaries, the putting himself in the place of those who had maligned him? Hitherto he had only felt that he was right and that they were wrong. He felt that still; he was as conscious as ever of the meanness and the poverty of their religious views. But now the meanness and the poverty of these views became to him a source not of repulsion but of attraction. He felt that they constituted the very cross which he was called to bear. He felt that without them he would be denuded of his participation in Christ's atoning work. How could he empty himself into the lives of others unless he were impressed with their emptiness? Was not his very aversion to the narrow and limited creed of his countrymen a ground for entering into sympathy with that creed? Was it not the very opportunity given him to take up the cross of his Lord, to put himself in the place of his opponents, and to impute to these opponents in the days of their broadened life the place he had himself acquired? Such was the thought of Paul, such was the germ of his later mellowness. He had received the spirit of the Master, and therefore he felt bound to receive the Master's ministry of reconciliation. Henceforth his work as an iconoclast was over, and his work as a reconstructor had begun. The gate was already ajar whose full opening was to reveal the length and the breadth of his developed Christianity. To the consideration of this process of subsequent expansion it will now be our province to turn.

CHAPTER IX.

THE FORESHADOWINGS OF A NEW DAY.

WE have now arrived at a point in Paul's spiritual history in which we seem to have reached a culmination. We have seen his Christian consciousness ripening from its dawn to its maturity. We have marked the growth of his spirit from its environment amid the Arabian solitudes to its emergence into the life and light of religious liberty. We have observed the process by which his mind passed from a Judaic into a Gentile Christianity, from the vision of a kingdom still in the future to the realisation of the truth that he was in possession of that kingdom here and now. We have considered the transition by which he advanced from the desire of personal reconciliation to the desire of being a personal reconciler, from the gazing on Christ's image to the participation in that image, from the justification by faith to the sanctification by love. And now the question which suggests itself is this, What more remains? Would it not seem as if the man had

climbed his highest, as if there were no further
height to gain ? Can there be any deeper depth of
Christianity than the bearing of Christ's image, and,
if a man has consciously reached that, can he get
nearer to the root of life ? In the epistles to the
Galatians, Corinthians, and Romans we have seen
Paul attaining this goal. What further progress
can any future writing reveal ? Must he not henceforth be content simply to hold his own, to occupy
the ground he has possessed, and dwell in the light
he has already conquered ?

And yet, a moment's reflection will convince us
that the most important stage of Paul's development
is still to come. If we were to express the matter
epigrammatically, and in language itself Pauline, we
should say that Paul had now reached the length
and depth of Divine love but not yet the breadth of
it. He had reached the *length* of Divine love ; he
had recognised the fact that the purpose of God in
Christ had stretched back beyond the limits of historical Christianity, and had embraced the history of
the Old Testament. He had reached the *depth* of
Divine love ; he had realised the truth that, in order
to be a follower of Christ, it was not enough to be
a partaker of His benefits, it was necessary to be a
distributer of His benefits. But there was one fact
he had not yet seen, and that was a vital fact—the
necessity that Christ's kingdom should be a power
embracing everything. He had felt its power within

himself; he had become conscious that he was animated by the identical spirit which dwelt in the
Master. But the very consciousness of this anima-
tion made him feel bound to be an ascetic. His first
Christian hope, as we have seen, had been the hope
of a new world, and this implied a despair of the old
one. This earlier form of asceticism had, indeed,
passed away. He had awakened to the truth that a
man might enter into Christ's life without dying,
and become a citizen of heaven while yet he trod
the earth. But to the mind of Paul this new thought
was as yet only the exchange of one form of asceticism for another. It seemed to him that, having
entered into the life of Christ, he was by that very
fact separated in the meantime from the life of the
world *as* a world. He no longer looked forward
to an absorption in a future kingdom, but he had
found an equally complete absorption in a kingdom
which had already come. He no longer dwelt on
the thought of a time when the world and its works
would be burned up; but if so, it was only because
to him the world and its works had been virtually
burned up already. The deepening of the new
Christian life had come to him with somewhat of
the same effect which had been produced upon his
physical eye by the shining of the light from
heaven: it had left in shadow a great portion of
that earthly scenery which of old had been to him
the glory of the universe.

The truth is, Christ to Paul did not yet "fill all things." He filled Paul's own world, but Paul's own world was as yet a very small thing; it did not stretch beyond the experiences of his religious consciousness. He had learned to sympathise with those beneath him; he had learned to make allowance for the wants of his weak brother. So far the life of Christ had to him been great gain. But it had not yet occurred to him that, to see Christ in all His fulness, he would require to reach a *wide* as well as a deep sympathy. It had not yet occurred to him that, if Christ was to be all in all, he would require to seek Him not only in the meagre faith of his weak brother but in that secular life of the world which to immediate perception revealed no faith at all. It was one thing, and a very grand thing, to have a spirit of Divine imputation whereby he was able to live in the experience of a brother less enlightened than himself, and to recognise beneath his shortcomings the glimmerings of a larger life; but it was another and a much higher thing to pass beyond the limits of what had hitherto been regarded as the realm of Christian brotherhood, and to recognise in the secular movements of a pagan world the preparation of many mansions in the house of the Father.

This was the day which was now about to dawn on the eyes of the Gentile apostle. He was about to enter into a new environment. Hitherto he had been environed successively by the atmosphere of Jerusalem and the atmosphere of Antioch ; he was now to be drawn within the influence of a larger atmosphere. The course of his journey was leading him step by step into proximity with that great city which constituted the centre of all civilisation—the metropolis of the Roman empire. As the shadow of that city broke upon his view, there broke also on his view another shadow—the vision of a kingdom which should incorporate all things. The vision of such a kingdom was inevitably suggested by the empire of the Cæsars. The design of that empire was incorporation. It aimed at universal dominion, but it aimed at a dominion whose universality should not crush the individual lives within its range. Its object was rather to appropriate than to annihilate the possessions of its enemies. It was willing to take within its Pantheon the gods of conquered nations, provided that these would submit to draw their inspiration from the Roman state. And the effect of this policy justified the expectation. The gods of conquered lands did not long occupy the Roman Pantheon without becoming Roman. In due time they lost their foreign character, became acclimatised to the soil on which they were bidden to dwell, and breathed the atmosphere of that empire to which originally their only attitude was subservience.

Such was the visible kingdom which first sug-

gested to the mind of Paul the defectiveness which
still hovered over his conception of the kingdom of
Christ. Why should the empire of Christ be less
incorporative than the empire of the Cæsars? If
an earthly and purely external power had been able
not only to incorporate but to acclimatise the
foreign elements of the world, ought not a power
professedly rooted in the deepest instincts of man's
spiritual nature to manifest the same universal influence? Was not the Messiah to receive the heathen
for His inheritance, and the uttermost parts of the
earth for His possession? Was it not the prerogative
of the kingdom of God that it should rule all things?
Did the Roman empire possess a power which was
denied to the Spirit of the Highest? If this purely
earthly force had been able by purely earthly means
to ingraft into itself all other forces of men, ought
not the power of the Divine Spirit to find also its
perfect manifestation in the union and blending of
its life with the lives of outer things?

It must not be imagined that this thought entered the mind of the apostle suddenly or abruptly.
The periods of natural development are in no case
marked off from each other by a distinct wall or
boundary-line. We have dates to indicate the time
when winter ends and spring begins, yet these dates
are purely artificial. There are days of spring in
the heart of winter, messengers which, like John
the Baptist, are sent in advance by the coming

year. The periods of human life are not abruptly
separated from one another. There is a nature of
the child and a nature of the man, yet the flashes of
the man prefigure themselves in the life of the
child. Like the grapes of Eshcol, the fruits of ripened development are borne beforehand into the
unripe age and exist as specimens of the time that
is to be. Spiritual life follows the same law. It
too has its seasons, and its fruits appropriate to each,
yet the fruits of the coming season always in measure reveal themselves amid the immaturities of the
earlier age. It was so with Paul. I have marked
out his epistles to the Galatians, Corinthians, and
Romans as distinguishing a special period in his
spiritual history—a period riper than the time which
went before and more uncultured than the time
which was coming. Yet, perhaps it may have
shown survivals of the past, and it certainly did
show anticipations of the future. The latest letter
of the group—that to the Romans—though it is still
within the boundary of the old, betrays already a
glimmering of the new. As the eyes of the apostle
became fixed on the great metropolis, the spirit of
that metropolis began to exert over him a mesmeric
influence. He was fascinated by the gaze, fascinated by the vision of something which seemed to
mimic in visible form the ideal of the Messianic
kingdom. He beheld the exhibition of a unity and
a universality which ought at least to have been

paralleled by the empire of Christ's religion. He was grieved that it had not been so paralleled. He was awakened into regret that Rome occupied alone a position of catholicity which the dominion of Christ should have shared with her. He set himself to inquire into the elements of this imperial greatness, set himself to consider whether such elements were at variance with the Christian ideal, and whether the Christian ideal might not appropriate them as her own.

He found that there were three elements which had fascinated and retained the hearts of the Gentile nations around this great centre of the world—the Roman ideal of law, the Roman ideal of power, and the Roman ideal of glory. Roman law was the most distinctive feature of the imperial greatness—the one feature which the empire has transmitted unimpaired to posterity, and by which she, being dead, yet speaketh. To the eye of Paul, the spectacle it presented must have been specially alluring. He saw what must have seemed to him an effort of the secular to imitate the sacred. Nowhere had the Gentile exhibited such a resemblance to the Jew. Rome had actually succeeded in doing what Judea had aspired to do; she had promulgated a series of enactments which were designed to rule the conduct of all the world. The question occurred to Paul in what light this mighty system of jurisprudence was to be regarded. Was not the Jewish

law ordained by heaven? If so, could this Roman
law be rooted and grounded in justice? Could any
system of human morality be allowed to rival the
influence of the Divine commandments; if Mount
Sinai had received the light, must not the Palatine
Hill occupy the shade? But to Paul thus meditating there rose a third alternative. Might not Mount
Sinai and the Palatine Hill be both manifestations
of a law from heaven? What if the theocratic commandments of Judea and the imperial enactments
of Rome had each come from the same source;
what if there was a law deeper than both, which had
embraced both and revealed both! Was there not a
commandment written in the heart, which was older
either than the summit of Mount Sinai or the city on
the top of the Palatine,—a commandment which had
its origin in the depths of human nature, and derived
its credentials from the writing of an invisible hand?

It was this inward questioning which led Paul to
a very remarkable conclusion, a conclusion which at
one time he would certainly have shrunk from arriv-
ing at. He had all along recognised the fact of the
inward authority of conscience, but he had hitherto
recognised that fact only in its relation to Christianity. Here, in this epistle to the Romans, and
under the strong influence of the Romans, he was
driven to take a wider view. There began to break
upon him the conviction that the inward law called
conscience had a purpose outside the present circle

of Christianity. There began to dawn on him the
thought that the Gentile had not, any more than the
Jew, been left without God in the world, that to
the one as much as to the other there had been a
preparatory legal training. He expresses this with
unfaltering confidence in his letter to the Christians
of the metropolis, "when the Gentiles, which have
not the law, do by nature the things contained in
the law, these, having not the law, are a law unto
themselves : which show the work of the law written
in their hearts, their conscience also bearing witness,
and their thoughts accusing or else excusing one
another." [1]   In these remarkable words Paul has
made a great advance in breadth of sentiment, has
revealed himself in a more distinct sense the apostle
of the Gentiles than ever he had done before.
Hitherto, he had been the Gentile apostle simply in
the sense that he proposed to offer them salvation
without passing through the gate of Judaism. He
here takes a bolder stand. He declares that the
Gentiles had received the offer of salvation by no
mere act of immediate grace, but on the ground of a
historical training. He says that they too, as much
as the children of Israel, had been led by the Divine
hand through a preparatory wilderness. To them,
as to the Jew, there had come a revelation of the
requirements of God ; the only difference had been
that while to the Jew it was written on tables of

[1] Rom. ii. 14, 15.

stone, to the Gentile it was inscribed on the tablets of the heart. In this recognition of the inherent and universal authority of conscience, Paul reached at a bound the idea of a natural religion; shall we not rather say, he reached at a bound the truth that the principle of the Christian life had its root in no merely Jewish soil but in the needs and aspirations of the universal heart of man?

The second element in the empire which attracted the eye of Paul was the Roman ideal of power. The Roman ideal of power was freedom. Other empires had based their aspiration on the attainment of a standard of mere mechanical force. The standard which Rome set before herself was not mechanical but mental. Her ideal of power was not the working of a mighty engine through the force of physical appliances; it was the impelling strength of a human will. What she valued above all things was the sense of mental unrestrainedness, the feeling that she could do what she liked. The idea of a paramount will, of a will which neither brooked nor received any contradiction in the achievement of its desires, was for her the pole-star which directed all her way; it was at once the goal to which she travelled and the light which helped her to travel. To the eye of Paul, marking the almost uninterrupted success with which that goal had been pursued Christianity must have presented for a moment a painful contrast. The watchword of Christianity was not power but service, her ideal was not a sovereign but a minister. In the vision of this self-sacrificing life, side by side with that spectacle of imperial life whose motive was unrestrained will, the apostle felt for a time as if the earth and the fulness thereof were not the Lord's. It is rather significant that it is in his epistle to the Romans we find him most confronted with that aspect of Christianity which suggested the idea of shame.[1] Elsewhere he speaks of its persecutions, of its hardships, of its outer and inner conflicts, of the watchings and fastings which its path involved. But here, in the presence of imperial Rome, all these difficulties of the Christian life are forgotten in the sense of a more absorbing difficulty—the trial of human pride. In the vision of service side by side with power, in the sight of ministration standing at the very doors of majesty, the apostle feels that his converts are incurring a greater danger than they could ever have experienced from the fear of martyrdom—the danger of being ashamed of a faith which seemed to isolate them from the prizes of human life.

What, then, is Paul's refuge under these circumstances? Does he decry the Roman element of power? Does he exalt the sense of shame as a means of impressing man with his own nothingness, and depreciate the possession of influence as a source of pride? None of these things. On the contrary,

[1] Rom. i. 16 ; v. 5.

his aim is rather to find a mitigation of the contrast between Rome and Christianity. Instead of trying to impress the world with the belief that the power acquired by the empire was a worthless thing, he seeks rather to show that, unconsciously to the empire herself, her power was really the result of the Christian principle. Wide as seemed the difference between the regal majesty of Rome and the sacrificial service of Christianity, Paul had awakened to the discovery that the majesty was founded upon sacrifice. Let any man read the sixth chapter of Romans and he will be convinced beyond controversy how thoroughly this thought had taken possession of the apostle's mind. In that chapter Paul virtually says: "You, Romans, boast of your freedom, and ye do well, but you have mistaken the source of your freedom. You imagine that you have derived it from the exercise of independence; it comes in fact from the intensity of your service. The reason why you are great as an empire is that you are dutiful as citizens. You have yielded yourselves into membership with a body-politic, and you have received back from the united organism the strength of that life which you have contributed to create. I tell you that there is no such thing as freedom *from* service; there is only freedom *in* service. If you want to be free from one law, you must embrace another law. If you would rise into empire over the things of the past, you must devote yourselves to some new and

o

fresh ideal. Your whole success as a political power
has been based upon such devotion, based upon your
self-surrender to the majesty of a thought to which
your contemporaries were deaf and blind. I, as a
Christian, seek no other method. I, like you, am in
search of a universal kingdom, but, unlike you, I recognise the truth that the founding of a universal
kingdom demands before all things a surrender to
the Will of the universe." [1]

The third element by which Paul was attracted in
the vision of the empire was the Roman ideal of
glory. The Roman ideal of glory was conquest; it
was that process of removing obstacles whereby the
sense of freedom was realised. As long as anything
was external to the empire it was a barrier to its advance. Accordingly, it became the goal of every
Roman citizen to transform the external into the
internal. Roman conquest consisted in laying hold
of those nations that stood outside the gates and
dragging them inside the gates. The only way to
realise the sense of freedom was to have nothing outside at all. The Roman empire was by no means
anxious nor even desirous to exterminate its enemies.
What it did desire was to transform its enemies into
national dependencies. It was quite willing that the
opposing nation should keep its manners, its religion,
and its laws, provided only it would consent to have
the Roman wall extended beyond its boundaries.

[1] Rom. vi. 12-18; compare viii. 2.

Its whole political policy, in short, alike in peace and war, consisted in a process of appropriation, by which it gathered into itself and transferred into its own service those very influences which in the days of old had been adverse to its life.

And here again to the eye of Paul there rose a striking parallel. There had been a time in which, as a Jew, he had looked upon the kingdom of God as something which could only exist by the extermination of the pains of life. There was a time in which he had held it to be impossible that the sufferings of human nature could be pressed into the service of God. We have seen how under the shadows of Arabia he had been oppressed by the thought of his own thorn. He had for the time found refuge from this oppression only by an appeal to the all-conquering strength of the Almighty, only by the reflection that the glory of God would be magnified in exalting him *in spite of* his weakness. This was a vision of conquest, but it was not a vision of Roman conquest; it was a subduing of suffering by an act of extermination. It proposed to destroy the enemies of the kingdom by putting them out of existence. There had not yet dawned on the mind of the apostle the vision of a kingdom of God whose enemies should be suppressed not by destruction but by incorporation, whose opposition should be conquered not by sweeping them off the face of the earth but by lifting them within the boundaries of the Divine empire.

That vision, that possibility, broke upon the eye of Paul only when he stood face to face with the spectacle of the Roman State. He there beheld the vision of an empire which had subdued its foes by utilising them, which had risen into strength by converting its enemies into members of its own body. And the thought occurred to Paul, ought not the kingdom of Christ to do the same? Why should not the all-conquering force of Christianity be also manifested by the utilising of those materials which had hitherto been deemed antagonistic to its progress? Hitherto, the religion of Christ had been glorified merely as a power which freed men from suffering; might it not be glorified as a power which freed men *through* suffering? Why should not the sorrows of life be themselves made the allies of the kingdom of God; why should not the cross become itself the crown? So Paul asked, and the answer appears in the epistle to the Church of that metropolis which had suggested the problem. Nowhere in previous epistles does his view of human suffering exhibit so roseate a hue.[1] It is no longer merely something from which he expects to be delivered; it is something which he expects, itself, to deliver him. It is no longer the prison-house from which he hopes that Christ will set him free; it is the key which unlocks the prison-house and ushers him into the glorious liberty of the sons of God.

[1] The nearest parallel is 2 Cor. iv. 17.

There is a ring of Roman triumph in such words as these—" We glory in tribulations also: knowing that tribulation worketh patience; and patience, experience; and experience, hope;"[1] and in those other words in which he expresses his permanent superiority to fear—" Who shall separate us from the love of Christ? shall tribulation, or distress, or persecution, or famine, or nakedness, or peril, or sword? Nay, in all these things we are more than conquerors, through Him that loved us."[2] It is "*in* all these things," not "over them." He has claimed for Christianity the Roman method of appropriation, of incorporation. He has asserted for Christ the right to rear an empire after the manner of Cæsar—by making friends of the once adverse forces, by transforming the weapons of the enemy into the defences of the kingdom.

Such are the evidences of that influence which the spectacle of the Roman empire was already beginning to exert over the mind of Paul. He was like the children of Israel standing on the borders of the promised land. Christianity had hitherto been to him a desert experience. It had been grand, but it had been solitary. In its latest development it had been something which had lifted Paul into a new world, but it had lifted him into an isolated world. He had been caught up to meet the Lord in the air, but for that very reason he had been separated from

[1] Rom. v. 3, 4. [2] Rom. viii. 35, 37.

the life of the common ground. Christ had become
to him not only a hope of glory, but a positive
glorification ; yet the glorification had been hitherto
purchased by leaving the lower world in the shade.
It had not occurred to Paul that Christ ought to
become the glory of the world *as* a world. It had
not occurred to him that the heavenly places of the
universe which remained to be filled were precisely
those places called mundane, precisely those haunts
of men which had been habitually assigned to the
Prince of the power of the air. But now there was
breaking upon the apostle's mind the first wave of
this great thought, and it was coming from the
shores of that empire which of all others had
mirrored most in its secularism the plan of the
kingdom of God. Paul there beheld the image of
a kingdom whose glory consisted precisely in its
incorporative or reconciling power. Reconciliation
had been for him the Christian watchword. But
when he saw the shadow of the Roman empire he
asked himself if he had been true to his watchword.
Had he not hitherto claimed too little for Christ ?
Was it enough that He should be the reconciler of
the soul ; ought He not also to be the reconciler of
the world ? Was it not His province to do for the
realm of spirit what Rome had done for the realm of
physical dominion—to find a field for its manifestation in the life of all secular things ? The vision of
Rome was to Paul the first-fruits of the promised

land. It came to him as a prophecy and presentiment of what was to constitute Christianity's highest glory, and in that sense of prophecy and presentiment he had already made his moment of transition from the Christ of the inward spirit to the Christ of the universal world.

CHAPTER X.

PAUL AND CHRISTIAN IMPERIALISM.

WE have now arrived at that stage of Paul's Christian experience in which it was to become a world-
experience.   Christ had hitherto been to him the all
of existence ; He was now to become the All " in all."
Up to this time He had been simply the secret of
Paul's life ; He was now to be revealed as the secret
of universal life, the presence and the power that
filled all things.   The steps by which this fulness of
Christ was realised were to be the steps of a descending ladder.   We have already seen that Paul's progress in the knowledge of Christ moved in a precisely opposite direction to that of the original apostles.   They began with the human Jesus, and had
to ascend to the conception of the Christ dwelling in
the heavens ; he began with the Christ dwelling in
the heavens, and had to descend to the thought of
the human Jesus.   His conception of Christ's union
with humanity had already been completed so far as
he was himself concerned, but it was still inadequate

as regarded the world. In his progressive descent
of the humanitarian ladder he had not yet reached
that step in which the Christian principle united
itself with the secular life. The religion which he
had left had been a theocracy, a rule of God over
the whole world. But the new religion had not as
yet to him become theocratic; it had hitherto only
ruled himself. The time was coming in which he
was to behold it in larger proportions, to discern its
wider scope, and to recognise its universal bearing.

The period of Paul's life which was to exhibit this
broader view of Christianity is that which compre-
hends the group of his epistles from the letter to the
Church of Philippi to the second letter to Timothy.
They may be called distinctively the epistles of the
captivity. With perhaps a partial and inconsider-
able break, the environment of Paul's subsequent
life was to be that Roman capital whose vision had
stimulated him into a wider spiritual path. He had
all along intended to visit Rome, but he had not
expected to reach it in the way in which he ultimately did. He had planned to come as a missionary; in point of fact he came as a prisoner. At first
sight it might appear that in this respect his missionary dream had been dispelled. It might seem
that to reach Rome as a prisoner was for him equivalent to not reaching Rome at all. He himself, at
all events, took the opposite view of this matter;[1]

[1] Phil. i. 13, and sequel.

he regarded his bonds as a gain.   Nor is it hard to
see that he had grounds for such congratulation.   The
man who had appeared as a political prisoner before
three Judean governors, and who had come to Rome
with the express purpose of vindicating the loyalty
of his faith before a criminal tribunal, was in a much
higher position of influence, notwithstanding his
bonds, than would have been occupied by an itinerant
Jewish missionary wandering after the counsel of his
will.   It is safe to affirm that such a missionary
would never have wandered into the focus of metropolitan power, never have seen Rome at its centre.
But, coming as a political prisoner, Paul came instantaneously into the centre.   He was brought into
the vicinity at once of the highest and of the lowest,
was placed in a position both to review and to be in-
terviewed.   His earliest influence fell precisely upon
that class which formed the nucleus of the empire—
the military.   In reaching the military, he put his
foot at once upon that ladder which communicated
with every grade of the Roman world, which led
upwards to the throne of the Cæsars and downwards
to the life of the populace.   Looking on that ladder,
Paul had a glimpse, in a moment, in the twinkling
of an eye, of the whole system of that wondrous
polity which had secured and retained the allegiance
of the world.

And in that glimpse of the Roman empire there
broke upon the mind of Paul a discovery which

exerted an important influence on all his subsequent
writings. He found that, notwithstanding the ladder
of communication between the heights and the depths
of the empire, there was in point of fact very little
communication itself. Rome had aimed at the establishment of a unity between all parts of the State.
But Paul found that the unity which had been attained was after all only an external one. The link
between the highest and the lowest was simply the
binding of an outward chain ; the highest never itself
came into actual contact with the lowest. Paul in
short discovered that the empire had a defect in its
own machinery, and precisely in that part of its mechanism of which it was most proud—the interpenetration of its members. He saw that in the deepest
sense there was no such interpenetration. He felt
that the empire was deficient in that very point at
which it had chiefly aimed, and he felt that Christianity alone could supply this deficiency. He had
come to Rome to defend his loyalty ; how could he
better accomplish this end than by indicating to the
Roman citizen the true mode of realising his own
ideal ?

That this thought passed through the mind of Paul
is to me evident from a passage written at an early
stage of his captivity. In one of the epistles of his
Roman imprisonment he thus speaks of Christ: "Now
that He ascended, what is it but that He also descended first into the lower parts of the earth ? He

that descended is the same also that ascended up far
above all heavens, that He might fill all things."[1]
I do not think these words can be adequately understood without reference to Paul's special environment. He was standing in the metropolis of the
world and looking at the world in its heights and
depths. Between its heights and its depths he saw
no communion. There were men that went up the
ladder and there were men that came down, but the
men who went up were not the same as the men that
came down. There were many instances of elevation
whereby the sons of the people reached the heights
of the empire, and there were many instances of
depression whereby the leaders of the empire were
precipitated to the level of the people. But to the
eye of Paul there did not present itself any instance
of a life, which had risen to the heights, voluntarily
descending again to the depths in order to elevate
his fellows. There were numberless illustrations of
successful ambition, of arduous climbing rewarded
by attainment of the goal. But the ambition never
seemed to pass into ministration. It did not strike
the man who had reached the goal that he had reached
it for a purpose, that the measure of his power was
the measure of his human responsibility. It did not
strike him that the attainment of personal power
was only valuable in so far as it opened up a road
to human helpfulness. There is no profit to the

[1] Eph. iv. 9, 10.

valleys in the mere fact of ascending to the mountains, unless the design of the ascent is a subsequent
descent, a communication to the valleys of the mountain light.

Such was the thought of Paul as through the
windows of his prison he surveyed the empire.
Now it seemed to him that Christianity could have
furnished an ideal which would have enabled the
Roman world to supply this defect, and I believe it
was this idea which prompted him to use the language
of the Ephesian epistle to which we have referred.
Divested of all figure and separated from all local
colouring, the passage seems to me to amount to this :
" In your metropolis there is no communication between the men who ascend and the men who descend,
and, because there is no communication, your own
ideal of empire is not realised. But we, Christians,
worship an ideal whose exaltation is only precious
because it is the result of a voluntary depression ; in
our empire the Man who goes up is the same Man
who once went down. We commemorate His ascension into power because He has ascended into a power
from which He once descended. He desired to fill
all things, to join the extremities of the social ladder.
In obedience to that desire He emptied Himself. He
came down into the haunts of human misery, of
squalor, of crime ; He made trial by contact of what
He had only known afar off. He had all along the
right to rule by power, but He desired to rule by

sympathy. He wished His government to be no arbitrary one but a government built upon the wants of men, responsive to those needs of the lowest which are the needs of all. He came down to learn these wants, and He has ascended only to give them effect. His ascension is the lifting up of humanity; He has carried into the highest the report of those things which are required by the lowliest; in the worship of His imperialism we commemorate the filling of all things."

Such is, I believe, a paraphrase of the thought which Paul meant to convey in this passage of Ephesians. It was dictated by a sense of that deficiency which he observed in the working out of the Roman ideal, by a desire to present the empire with a new and higher ideal which, even while transcending its own, would enable its own to be realised. Paul meant to suggest that, if men would take the Christian ideal as their standard of heroism, they would themselves be constrained to repeat the same process of ministration. His aim is not to inculcate a dogma ; it is to inspire a common life. In a passage which, whether written earlier or later, is almost contemporaneous, he expresses this aim still more pronouncedly. "Let this mind be in you," he says, "which was also in Christ Jesus." He then goes on to tell his hearers what mind it was that he desires to be in them. He describes the history of that mind as the history of a descent from the high-

est height of power to the lowest depth of humiliation. He traces its downward course step by step
until it reaches the common ground where all life
claims brotherhood,—from the form of God to the
form of an angelic servant, from the form of an
angelic servant to the likeness of a man, from the
likeness of a man in his glory to the fashion of a
man in his transitoriness, from the shifting fashion
of the human to the final stage of the mortal—
death. And then, having brought the Son of man
to this lowest ground of abasement, the Jewish captive turns round and addresses his captors. He declares that their imperialism was excelled by the
majesty of the Crucified. He declares that, not in
spite of but by reason of this humiliation, He had
risen into a height of empire before which theirs
must bow, " Wherefore God hath highly exalted Him,
and given Him a name that is above every name:
that to the name of Jesus every knee should bend, of
things in heaven, and things in earth, and things
under the earth."[1]

What did Paul mean to teach the Roman world
by the presentation of such an ideal ? Nothing less
than a new model of government, a model which,
without one change in its existing constitution,
might instantaneously become its own. He meant to
tell it that hitherto it had failed to realise, failed to
utilise, the resources of its own dominion, that its

[1] Phil. ii. 5-10.

empire was smaller in extent and less powerful in regal authority than it ever ought to have been. It had sought to bind together the fragments of the world from without; the only certain bond was a union from within. There was no empire whose extent could be compared to the empire of the heart; he who should conquer that, was king indeed. But he who would conquer that, must stoop to the uttermost, nethermost. He must come down to those common wants which lie at the base of all life, and which, because they lie at the base, are alone fitted to be the binding chain of humanity. At the middle of the ladder men cannot be united; the wants there are artificial, and they are exchanged hour by hour. But at the foot the wants of men are common and permanent. Hunger, thirst, cold, weariness, moments of isolation, forms of poverty, imminent shadows of death, are absent from no special caste, and are found at all times. They are felt by Cæsar as much as by his household. What if Cæsar could be brought to feel them *for* his household! What if his position at the top of the ladder, instead of removing him above the cries of the multitude, should bring him more into contact with these cries! What if, just because he stood on the height, he were made in a special sense susceptible of impressions from below, in a special sense recipient of the plaints and sorrows of the valleys beneath!

It is at this stage, at this moment when the sins

and sorrows of the empire are pressing on his mind, that there breaks upon the view of the apostle what I cannot otherwise describe than as a new thought—a thought which amounts to nothing less than the discovery of an outer membership in the body of Christ. From the days when he wrote his first epistle to the Corinthians, the figure which he had adopted to express the communion between Christ and His people was the idea of that connection which subsists between the head and the members of a human body. The headship of Christ had become to him a dearer expression than the kingdom of Christ, and there is no wonder. For the head of a body is a conception not only different from, but in some respects the reverse of, the king of a state. The king of a state rules by giving his impressions *to* the members; the head of a body rules by receiving its impressions *from* the members. The king governs by commanding; the head in one sense may be said to reign by obeying. The king is the first mover and the members are his servants; the head only begins to act after the communication of the members, and may be called the servant of all. It is not surprising, therefore, that to the mind of Paul this latter figure should have become a peculiarly endearing symbol for expressing the relations of the communiontable. To be a member of Christ's body was to make Christ recipient of all those impressions of pain which existed in the heart of the creature;

His capacity for headship was itself His capacity for suffering.

In all this there was nothing new to Paul. It was the thought which had dominated his mind since the second period of his Christian life—that period in which he began to realise eternity not merely as an existence of the future but as an existence of the present hour. But now, standing under the shadow of the Roman empire, there flashes upon his mind a thought which certainly seems to me an addition to his past experience. Hitherto, the membership in Christ's body had been viewed by him simply in its relation to the Church. In his epistles to the Ephesians and Colossians a new leaf is added to the communion-table, and he declares, almost in so many words, that the members of the state are also parts of the body of Christ. In these epistles he appears to me for the first time to extend the sacramental relation from the inner to the outer court of the tabernacle. I base this opinion not upon his recognition of Christ's Messianic reign over the nations; that was an idea as old as Judaism itself. But the point here is, that the Messianic reign itself is represented as a bodily burden-bearing. Christ bears the pains not only of the members but of those things which the members have touched. There is a sacramental continuity established between the Church and the world, so that He who carries the burdens of the Church carries the burdens of the world too. "He gave Him to be head over all things;"[1] "Ye are complete in Him, which is the head of all principality and power."[2] Let us observe what is implied in this language. Nothing less than the clothing of secular royalty in a new and sacrificial symbol. Hitherto, headship had been the prerogative of the priest; it was now declared to be the prerogative of the king. In the eyes of the Roman world, in the eyes of prætor, proconsul, senate, emperor, there is flashed the image of a kingdom not before seen amongst the Gentiles, not before seen amongst the Jews,—a kingdom whose characteristic is service, whose watchword is priesthood, whose sceptre is sacrifice, and whose strength of power is the weight of its burden-bearing.

Such is the new figure of empire which breaks forth in those writings of St Paul that bear the impress of the Roman captivity. Foreshadowed in the epistle to the Romans, promulgated in the epistle to the Ephesians, and reiterated in the epistle to the Colossians, it becomes henceforth not only the centre of his religious thought but the root of his humanitarian sympathy. Sacrifice takes a new and a higher place in his system. It is no longer merely the cloud which obscured for a time the empire of the Son of man; it is itself the empire of the Son of man, the source of His authority, the sceptre of His throne. It is no longer

[1] Eph. i. 22.　　　　　　[2] Col. ii. 10.

simply the impediment which must be got rid of
ere the kingdom shall come; it is itself the coming
of the kingdom.[1]   The exaltation of Christ is henceforth with Paul not the conquest but the result of
His cross.   If He has received a name before which
every knee must bend, it is because He Himself has
bent the knee to humanity.   To crown Christ simply
as a king is to crown Him on the ground that He
has risen above the circumstances of human pain
and human weakness; but to crown Him as the
head is to put the diadem on His brow on precisely
the opposite ground—on the ground that human pain
and weakness have become universally His own.

In assigning to the Son of man this transformed
ideal of government, Paul was really idealising it
for all time.   In the precincts of his lonely dungeon
he was effecting a greater revolution than he had
wrought through all his missionary labours.   He
was putting into the hearts of men a thought that
was to germinate and grow.   Quite unconsciously
to himself, he was at that hour the maker of modern
history.   He was weaving a conception of empire
which was destined to captivate and to dominate
the human mind.   He was striking the first decided
blow at dominions, and principalities, and powers,—
at every form of government in which the will of
the individual had aspired to obliterate the will of
the community.   He was occupying the position of

[1] Cf. Col. i. 11.

a political protestant. He was advocating the right of each man to be an integral part of the state, proclaiming the duty of each sovereign to bear the burdens of those beneath him. He did not propose such a goal as a limit to imperialism but as an extension of the boundaries of empire. He proposed it as the highest conceivable kind of government, as the only kind of government which would ultimately exert a universal and a permanent sway. If he had offered the suggestion in the interest of a democracy, it would inevitably have perished at its birth; it would have been crushed by the power of the Cæsars. But when he offered it as a wreath to his own Divinity, when he proclaimed it as a thought which he would like to see realised in the empire of the Son of man, he immediately disarmed all criticism. He was presenting to the imperial world an ideal of government constructed in its own interests, constructed with a view to the enlargement and consolidation of the title of king. He was assigning this ideal to no earthly potentate but to the Being whom he himself worshipped as Divine. To the Roman world, therefore, his attitude was the reverse of revolutionary. Nay, that world had already in some sense been prepared for the new evangel. The idea was half in the air. His theory of government was to the Latins what his sermon on Mars' Hill was to the Greeks, —an amplification of that thought after which they

had been seeking, and whose imperfection had impeded their own progress. Seneca had but recently
told his Roman countrymen that they were members
of a Divine body; Paul put a head upon the body
and made it human.

From this time forth the Christian creed became
in its essence humanitarian. It had all along been
so in its practice. On the lips of the Divine Founder Christianity had taken the form of a religion
adapted to the wants of man as man; His own
favourite name had been the Son of man. With
the dawn of theological systems there had come the
danger of a limitation; the servants of Christ had
for a time been separated from the common earth
and placed on a mountain apart. But with the
realisation of this new thought heaven and earth
again met together. To say that Christ was the
head of principalities was to give Him a far
wider range than merely to say that He was the
head of the Christian body. As the head of the
Christian body He could only come into contact
with man in his religion; as the head of principalities He came into contact with man in his
manhood. The inner circle of membership still
remained, but an outer circle was added to it.
There was still a communion of faith wherein the
Master met in an upper room with His disciples;
but in addition to this there was another communion wherein the Master came into contact with

those who were not His disciples—a communion in which He met the multitude in the desert, and broke the bread to them on the ground of their hunger alone. To sit at the head of the inner table was to have communion with man on the ground of his religious affinity. But to sit at the head of the outer table was to have communion with man on the ground of his being a creature. It was to stoop beneath the sphere of religious affinity into the sphere of nature. It was to become the high priest of the uncircumcised, of the unclean, of the unredeemed. It was to become affected with want because it *was* want. It was to take up into His sympathy the great fact of sorrow, irrespective of its origin and independently of its cause, to incorporate sufferings which perhaps were even now the fruit of sin, and which, just because they were sufferings, had become the prerogative of royalty. Therefore, in this bold figure of secular headship we have the dawn of a humanitarian Christianity—a dawn whose full unfolding was perhaps invisible even to the apostle himself, but which yet bore within it the germ of boundless possibilities. The conception of God's kingdom which it suggested was one which was to bear fruit undreamt of in the philosophy of that time, one which was to influence the course of future governments and to turn into new channels the stream of old faiths. It was one of the most silent movements in the whole history of man, yet it set in motion a train of consequences whose force is not yet expended and whose issues are still un-realised.

But, what we are here concerned with is the effect of the new conception on the mind of Paul himself. We have seen that the history of Paul's mind has been hitherto the history of a development in which the spirit of the man has descended from the heavenly to the earthly sphere. We have seen how, beginning with the vision of the glorified Christ, and finding, therefore, his first Christian ideal in the thought of something which transcends the earth, he has yet been step by step descending the Jacob's ladder. Starting with the Divine and superhuman, we have found him approaching ever nearer to the mundane and the earthly. The goal towards which he tended was, as I have said, precisely the opposite of that which was the goal of the other apostles. Their starting-point was to be his landing-place. They looked first upon the human Christ and thence rose up to the Divine; he looked first upon the Divine Christ and thence came down to the human. He began with the Christ of resurrection, the life that had risen above the changes of the world. His original theology, therefore, bore a character corre-sponding to such a vision; it dealt with themes which were rather intellectual than practical, rather speculative than utilitarian. But in proportion as he approached the starting-point of the first disciples, in proportion as he came into contact with the traces of Christ's human ministry, his own teaching became more human. It was not that he changed his system; it was rather that he saw a new and wider application for his system. He perceived that the doctrine and work of the Master had a wider bearing than he had originally supposed, that they were not simply tokens of admission into another world but means for managing the affairs of this. He perceived that the deepest power of the Gospel lay in its adaptation to present need, in its provision for the wants of the hour, in its capacity to support the burdens of earthly life. To him, in short, Christianity was ever more and more revealed as a secular force, the most powerful and influential of all secular forces — a force which had its province in the commonplace duties of the day, and which must find its consummation in the civilising of the united world.

Such is the order of Paul's development—a development from the celestial to the mundane. There are times in the history of every man in which the order of his development is quickened. There are moments of acceleration in which the natural fruit of years is compressed into the growth of months. Such a moment had now come for Paul. His course, hitherto, had been steadily towards the earthly and the human, but it was now to be rapidly so. The crisis of his life was his Roman captivity. It placed him in an instant at the very centre of the world's movement and showed him man in all his phases. It revealed to him the need of a larger and a wider scheme of salvation than he had hitherto conceived. It taught him the necessity of a contact between the Divine and the human based on broader lines than those of assimilation, a contact which should have its ground not alone in the creature's faith but in the creature's need. It led him to the conclusion that man's claim to the Divine sustenance is not his fulness but his emptiness. It showed him that the ultimate meeting-place between the Infinite and the finite was the creature's sense of want, and that, in the power to come into contact with this want, the kingdom of God had passed from the empire of sovereignty into the empire of headship.

Here, then, is the task which now lies before us— to unfold the steps of that process by which Paul realised the full scope and bearing of this new conception. " Unfold " is, indeed, the most appropriate word. The idea of government at which Paul had now arrived was already an all-embracing idea; it comprehended within itself the minutest details of secular life, and there was no limit to its far-reachingness. But just on this account its full scope could not at once be seen—not even by the man who had conceived it. To the mind of Paul, as we have seen, the idea at first came only in its religious garb, or, to speak more correctly, in a garb distinguished from the world. Like everything else in his development, this thought had to work downwards, had to descend from the skies to the plains. It was originally no more than the ideal of a heavenly life, a life worth admiring and worth aspiring to. Paul did not at once perceive that if a man came to admire that heavenly life, there would be a transformation of all secular life. He did not at once perceive that such an idea as the headship of Christ could not be anything without being everything, could not take possession of the throne of theology without influencing and dominating the most common affairs of the passing hour. It was one by one that to the eye of Paul this idea of the Divine headship was seen embracing the circles of everyday experience. He beheld it gradually descending from the height to the plain and from the plain to the valley, until it comprehended in the sweep of its downward movement the minutest and most trivial incidents in the life of the individual man.

How are we to trace the steps of this development? How shall we determine the order in which Paul realised the applications of this new idea of government? We have from his hands four epistles of the first captivity—those to the Philippians, Ephesians, Colossians, and Philemon. We cannot tell with any confidence in what order these were written, nor, if we could, would it much avail us. In whatever order they come, they are almost contemporaneous. The distance between them can be

measured at most only by a few months. Between
the earliest and the latest there does not intervene
space enough to justify us in seeking in them stages
of comparative development. We must abandon,
therefore, any hope of tracing the order of Paul's
later stages by determining the sequence of these
epistles. But there is another source of suggestion
open to us. There is a peculiarity common to nearly
all the writings of St Paul. Each epistle consists of
two parts—one doctrinal and the other practical, and
the doctrinal invariably comes first. Why does the
doctrinal come first? Why does the discussion of
things in heaven precede the direction towards
things on earth? Modern usage would certainly
reverse the process. The inductive method of
science has taught men to begin with matters of
personal observation and thence to ascend to the
theoretical and the abstract. But Paul was not a
modern; he was a scion of the stock of Abraham,
and he retained even in his Christianity the traditions
of his nation. These traditions pointed in an exactly
opposite direction to the modern method of induc-
tion; the Jew began with God and thence he descended to man. Moreover, as we have seen, Paul's
own development had been in this and not in the
modern direction. His earliest vision had been a
vision of the things above, not of the things on the
earth; it was precisely here that his experience had
been distinguished from the experience of contem-

porary apostles. Is it strange that the method of
his life should have become the method of his
thought? Is it strange that the steps of that order
which he had described in his own experience should
have become the steps of that order in which he
beheld the unfolding of all things? His own spiritual history had been a progress from heaven to
earth; was not the progress from heaven to earth
the natural course in which he should realise the
fulness of every doctrine?

Accordingly, in considering the development of the
thought in these later epistles, we shall adopt this
order which we have found in the mind of Paul himself. Wherever he speaks of Christ's headship in its
theological or abstract bearings, we shall assume that
we are dealing with the thought in its earlier aspect,
in that aspect in which it first presented itself to his
mind. Wherever, on the other hand, he speaks of
the headship of Christ in its earthly or human relations, wherever he deals with it in its reference to
social or domestic problems, we shall take it for
granted that the idea has presented itself to him in
its later or more developed form. We shall thus
preserve the analogy of that development which we
have found everywhere else in the spiritual life of
this apostle, and shall see him at the end, as we have
seen him at the beginning, unfolding in the order of
his thought, from the vision of Christianity on the
height to the vision of Christianity in the vale.

CHAPTER XI.

PAUL AND THE UNIVERSE.

I NOW proceed to unfold the order of that development by which the mind of the Gentile apostle applied to life's different phases the new idea of Divine government. In accordance with the principle stated in the previous chapter, I shall look for the steps of that development in the descent from the Divine to the human. I shall seek first of all for any modification which this thought exerted on the apostle's view of the universe at large, and afterwards I shall endeavour to find the traces of its influence in any modification of his attitude towards the common things of earth and time.

What, then, was Paul's view of the universe at this stage of his pilgrimage? Naturally speaking, it ought to have been a very black one. He was a captive in chains. He had been interrupted in his missionary labours. His work had been seemingly brought to a close at the very moment when he was beginning to prosper. He had been placed in the

most thoroughly unsympathetic atmosphere which
had ever yet environed him—an atmosphere in which
he had neither the geniality of friendship to cheer
nor the warmth of enmity to stimulate, but simply
the chill of cold indifference. Opposition is a form
of sympathy; it indicates that a man's views are at
least an object of interest. But indifference is the
absence of all interest either repulsive or cohesive;
it is the simple negation of sympathy between one
mind and another, and therefore it is the most solitary atmosphere which any mind can occupy. Such
was Paul's atmosphere in Rome. He had passed beyond the reach either of praise or censure, either of
friends or foes. He had neither the admiration of
his Gentile converts nor the malignity of his Jewish
adversaries; he had simply the unintelligent gaze of
a new world which did not understand him. If there
ever was a time in which Paul might have thought
darkly of the possibilities of life, it was now. If
there ever was a time in which we should expect
him to take a gloomy view of the universe, it would
be in these days when he was writing his Ephesian
and Colossian epistles. And yet we shall find that it
is precisely in these days that his view of the possibilities of life becomes wider and brighter. The
period of Paul's life which of all others is most
joyous is the period of the Roman captivity. There
is a freedom and a conviction about his utterances
at this time which goes beyond the force of all his

previous utterances. His hope is more abounding, his view more large, his joy more spontaneous. It seems as if a weight were lifted, as if a source of oppression were removed. And we shall find that this elevation of spirits was not something aimless or arbitrary; it came from an elevation of standpoint. The brightening of his own sky resulted from a brightening of the universal sky, from a more sanguine conception of the possibilities of creation at large. Let us briefly consider the direction in which this clearing of the atmosphere appeared.

Two extreme views have been held as to the nature of this universe—that of the optimist and that of the pessimist. The former is represented by the state religion of the Chinese empire; the latter by the creed of ancient Buddhism. The Chinaman looks upon this world, in so far as it is contained within the bounds of his dominion, as having already reached the limit of perfection and surpassed the necessity for improvement. The Buddhist looks upon this world as being in its very nature a scene of misery, incapable of being improved and unable to be transcended. I have called these the extremes, because they represent to their full extent the opposite views of the universe. There are many intermediate shades between them, approximating either to the one side or to the other; but nowhere else is either view expressed with such uncompromising force. The nearest approach to the Chinaman is the

Jew. His view of the world was, on the whole, optimistic. He moved between two golden suns; he had a paradise in the past and a paradise in the future. Latterly, he had a paradise also in the present. He came to believe in the possibility of justification by law, in other words, of being made perfect by the successful observance · of a series of national statutes. When he had reached such a thought as this, his optimism was equal to, and analogous to, the optimism of the Chinese empire.

Paul, being a Jew, and a Jew of the later age, shared at first in the optimism of his country and his time. We have his own warrant for saying that he originally believed in the inherent perfectibility of human nature. The law was once to him what it was to his countrymen—a ladder on which the human soul might climb from earth to heaven. When he embraced Christianity he abandoned this sense of present optimism; he ceased to believe that the law was adequate even to convert, much less to perfect, a human soul. The immediate effect of his Christianity was to drive him into an opposite extreme. At no time, indeed, did he ever become a pessimist in the absolute sense. At no time did he abandon his Jewish conviction that there was coming in the future an age of purest gold whose splendour would dispel the present darkness and usher in the reign of the Messiah's kingdom. Yet, at first to the mind of Paul there was no connection between the coming age of gold and the present age of iron. If he was an optimist for the future, he was on that very account a pessimist for the passing hour. It seemed to him that the only value of the hour lay in the fact that it *was* passing. In giving up the possibility of justification by law he seemed to have given up everything that made present life worth possessing. The trials and struggles of the common day presented themselves as barriers that must be overcome ere the day of the Lord should dawn—things which ought, indeed, to be borne with patience, but whose only virtue consisted in the lesson of patience which they taught. The sufferings of this life, so far as this life was concerned, had as yet revealed no value. His eye contemplated them only in their relation to a state of existence before whose glory they would pass away. Even in that passage which, of all others in his earlier epistles, comes nearest to the recognition of a remedial element in sorrow (2 Cor. iv. 17, 18), the remedial element is made to depend for its recognition on the contemplation of the objects which are above, " while we look not to the things which are seen, but to the things which are not seen." The reason is plain. Paul had as yet looked only on the unseen realities. He had hitherto viewed the Gospel of Christ only in its relation to a life incorruptible, undefiled, and unfading ; and therefore he could at first contemplate the sorrows of life only in their bearing on this great beyond. His vision was perfectly true, but it was not yet full; it was just and accurate, but it did not embrace all the scene. That the sufferings of life had a bearing on the future world was true, but they had also a bearing on the present world. Paul had seen the one half of the landscape and it was the higher half; but the lower half remained to be seen, and without it the vision of Christ's kingdom was not complete.

That vision was to be completed in the Roman captivity. It found its beginning in that new conception of the kingdom of God which contemplated the Messiah not as the sovereign of a state but as the head of a body. The doctrine of the secular headship of Christ transfigured the whole aspect of earthly sorrow. If the empire of Christ consisted in His power to bear the infirmities of the bodily members, if His highest strength was manifested in His capacity to receive those impressions of pain which the bodily members bore, it followed beyond all question that the sorrows of this present life had themselves an optimistic bearing. They were no longer merely the penalties of past transgression, they were no longer even merely the training for a state of glory ; they were themselves a state of glory. They were at the present moment, now and here, the direct and immediate source of that empire and dominion which the Messiah already wielded, and were to be in the future the source of that dominion which was yet to be added to His sway. Paul does not scruple to declare that the Messiah's earthly kingdom was only lacking in perfection because it was lacking in its full amount of suffering, and that, when it reached its complete incorporation of human sorrow, it would reach its perfect empire over the hearts of men.[1]

Accordingly, if at this latter stage Paul had been asked his opinion of the present system of things, his answer would have been different from what it would have been in earlier days. In earlier days he would have pronounced the present system of things to be either absolutely good or absolutely bad according to the state of his own experience. In the stage immediately preceding his conversion his attitude would have been optimistic; in the stage immediately following that event his tendency would have been pessimistic. In both cases, however, his view would have been determined by the belief that the present system of things was already a completed quantity, that the world as it now stands is finished. But when he had reached the days of the Roman captivity this was precisely the belief which had been shaken. He had come to the conclusion that the present world is not a finished structure, that it is only a structure in the process of building. He would have deprecated any judgment as to its ultimate deformity on the ground of its actual appearance. He would

[1] Col. i. 24.

have done so precisely for the same reason that he would have deprecated any criticism of a physical building while it was in the act of its formation. He knew that the building stage was of necessity a stage of deformity and apparently a stage of confusion. He attributed the seeming inequalities of the world to the fact that the world was not completed, that it was only in process of growth. " All the building, fitly framed together, *groweth* unto an holy temple in the Lord," [1] " the whole body fitly joined together and compacted by that which every joint supplieth, *maketh increase* unto the edifying of itself in love," [2] are the words in which he expresses his sense of the present position of things. He has come to contemplate the scenes of time as the scenes of an unfinished drama, whose present aspect may be grievous and whose actual manifestation leaves much to be desired, but which yet can only be judged with reference to a concluding act towards which they are hastening, and to whose climax they are unconsciously contributing.

It will be seen, then, that at the period of the Roman captivity Paul's attitude towards the world, as a world, had been reversed. He had ceased to view it merely as a foil to bring out the resistance of the kingdom of God ; he had come to look on it as itself an essential part of that kingdom, one of the rooms in the many mansions of the Father. There

[1] Eph. ii. 21.   [2] Eph. iv. 16.

is another point, however, to which I wish to invite
attention, a point of not less clearness and of still
greater importance. The doctrine of the secular
headship of Christ not only opened up to Paul a
more optimistic view of the universe; it would hardly
be too much to say that it first revealed to him the
universe itself. It did for him very much what
the telescope does for the man of science. In one
respect the telescope has enlarged our vision of the
field of nature; but, paradoxical as it may seem,
there is another respect in which it has made our
universe smaller. It has caused us to experience
somewhat of that feeling which we get by travelling
—that the circle of life is not so big as we thought
it was, and that the things abroad are unexpectedly
related to things at home. If the telescope has
widened our sense of the universe's vastness, it has
lessened our sense of its variety. It has everywhere
simplified and minimised the materials of actual
existence. It has shown us that the laws which
operate in our globe are operative through all space.
It has taught us that there is an analogy between
all the works of nature from the least unto the
greatest. It has made us aware that, while "star
differeth from star in glory," it is the difference not
of kind but of degree, and that the life of the small-
est is supported by the same great principle which
regulates the being of the largest. Above all, it has
revealed to us the fact that between the remotest

points of space there is stretched a cord of continuity by which the extremities of creation are joined and the many are made one—a cord which binds together things that were once thought to have no affinity, and makes it impossible to touch a part without directly affecting the whole. It is here that specially Paul's new conception of the system of nature carried with it a telescopic effect. It was the discovery of a principle of continuity, of a cord by which things were bound together which had once seemed heterogeneous. It was the awakening to the knowledge that the system of nature is not a series of isolated objects, but a connected and united universe, a life which circulates, indeed, through endless varieties and manifests itself in numberless forms, but which through all vicissitudes and through all variations preserves an unbroken unity and retains a common element. This was the great fact which burst upon the mind of the Gentile apostle when he conceived this new idea of Divine government, and I now proceed to consider the nature of that change which it produced upon his view.

The popular notion is that the conception of the universe entertained by the Jewish nation is in itself more favourable to the religious life of man than the conception of the universe which has been prevalent since the days of Copernicus. The idea is entertained that the belief in the earth as the centre of the universe is naturally and necessarily calculated to increase man's faith in the providential care of a Supreme Intelligence. And yet I think a deeper reflection will tend at least greatly to modify this view. I have no doubt indeed that, other things being equal, the belief in the earth's centrality was a factor favourable to faith. But the qualifying clause is a most important one. Provided those parts of the universe which lie above and below the centre are analogous in their nature to the parts embraced within the centre, I should concede at once that the Ptolemaic system of astronomy would lend itself to religion better than the Copernican. But if, on the other hand, the Ptolemaic system of astronomy, while regarding this earth as the centre of the universe, looked upon the centre as having no resemblance to the circumference, the matter would wear a very different aspect. I should say that in this case the Copernican system of astronomy, supplemented by the gravitation theory of Newton, was an infinitely higher aid to religious belief. Although in this modern system the earth is no longer the centre of the universe, the universe has itself become analogous to the earth ; one common law binds the highest and the lowest, and, what is more important, binds the highest *to* the lowest. There may be a measureless distance between the earth on which I stand and the central point of the universal system, but through that distance there stretches one and the same law connecting the phenomena of my life with the phenomena which prevail at the centre. There is, in short, in the universe of our modern thought an established line of communication between the system of nature at its apex and the system of nature at its base, and by the existence of that line of communication the apex and the base are proved to be, in their nature, one.

Now, in the later Judaism, the system contemplated in the outer world was precisely the reverse of this. It is true that there as elsewhere the earth was viewed as the centre of the universe, and that to this extent man had an advantage in realising the presence of a providential care. But then, there was a great gulf fixed between the centre and the apex—between man and God. I do not speak of a gulf of spatial distance; that conception is unavoidable in any view of nature which reaches the standard of intelligence. But the difference between God and man in the developed stage of Jewish theology was practically a difference not simply of degree but of kind. If the God of that theology had been merely the first in a series of intelligences, however vast in its gradations that series might be, there would still have always existed a line of communication between the extremest parts of the universe. But the God of Jewish theology was not the first of a series; He was a life separated from all the rest of the series. He not only was without a rival but without a second. It was His essence to be alone,

His nature to be incommunicable. In the conception of the Jew, God would have ceased to be God if He had dwelt in any other light than a light which was inaccessible. The fulness of His glory consisted expressly in His inaccessibility, lay precisely in the fact that no man could see His face and live. And the reason why the Jew attributed to the Creator this isolation from the creature was his contempt of creature life. The whole creation was in a state of suffering, and it was in a state of suffering because it was in a state of sin.[1] To the mind of the Jew, suffering was inseparable from sin. He did not, indeed, regard it as outside the Divine government, but it was within that government only as a form of penal infliction. To attribute, therefore, a participation in suffering to God was in his view blasphemous; it was tantamount to denying the Divine majesty. It was imperative that the associations of Divinity and sorrow should be kept for ever apart, lest the purity of the Infinite garment should be sullied by contact with corruption. Accordingly, to the mind of the Jew, God was a Being who dwelt alone. It was in the interest of His holiness rather than in the interest of His greatness that he assigned Him this solitude. He felt that, if creature-life was a life of suffering, and if a life of suffering was the fruit of sin, there could be no direct intercourse between the creature and the Creator; there must be

---

[1] Cf. Rom. viii. 20, and sequel.

fixed an eternal and impassable chasm between the
Divine Life at the apex of the universe and the most
saintly human life that inhabited the centre.

The question was, How was this chasm to be filled?
However much God was alone in His nature, He was
to the Jew perpetually present in His action on the
affairs of men. If on the one hand it was imperative to preserve the conception of His unspotted
holiness, it was on the other no less necessary to
keep undimmed the impression of His theocratic
power. How was God at one and the same moment
to be a Presence dwelling alone in the solitude of His
own perfections, and a Power active and operative
in the affairs of human life? Such was the problem
which presented itself to the mind of the later Judaism—the filling of that vast chasm which the infin-
itude of the Divine holiness had seemed to interpose
between the centre and the summit of the universe
of being.

And the later Judaism made an effort to solve
that problem. It proposed to fill up the chasm between man at the centre and God at the apex by
means of a hierarchy of celestial intelligences, a ladder of intermediate beings descending in order of
their perfection from the highest archangel to the
lowliest of those ministering spirits who inhabited
the region immediately above the human. On the
steps of this vast descent came the messages both
from above and from below, the announcement of

the will of God to man and the announcement of
the needs of man to God. On these steps rose the
prayers of the human to the Divine, on these descended the answers of the Divine to the human.
There was no direct communication, there was no
immediate communion, but there was established
what seemed to be an equivalent for the want of
these—a gradation of finite intelligences ever reaching nearer the ultimate goal.

I say "what seemed to be," for in reality the filling of the chasm was only in appearance. There
was no real gradation established between the life
of the Creator and the life of the creature. The
distance between the apex and the centre of the universe was not bridged by one hair's-breadth. It was
easy to stretch in fancy a stair of communication
between the intelligence nearest to man and the
intelligence nearest to the Divine; but when the
latter point was reached the chasm remained infinite
still. Between the Divine and the intelligence
nearest to the Divine there was as great a sphere
of separation as existed before the attempt was made
to fill it. Man in his earthly centrality remained
as much divorced from God in His solitary perfection as he had been without the intervention of
celestial spirits, and the intervention of these celestial spirits, useless as it was to bridge the gulf,
became simply a cumbrous appendage to the recognised objects of theological thought.

Now, Paul was a child of the later Judaism, and shared in all the intensity of its problems. He came into the world at a time when his countrymen had made a full trial of the intervention of celestial spirits. Paul himself had shared in that belief of his nation and had found it wanting. I believe he found it wanting even before he became a Christian, and that a sense of its want was one of the factors which impelled him towards Christianity. But there is no doubt at all that after he became a Christian the belief in these celestial mediators was one of the greatest hindrances to his religious communion. One has only to read his later epistles in order to see how much his mind was troubled by the thought of "principalities and powers" intervening between himself and his God; they had been originally a source of strength, but they were now an element of weakness. Even so early as in his epistle to the Romans we find him exclaiming, "I am persuaded, that neither angels, nor principalities, nor powers, shall be able to separate us from the love of God." One wonders at first sight why such things *should* separate from the love of God. We are tempted originally to suppose that Paul is speaking of wicked spirits, of the emissaries of Satan. Yet, in truth, it is not so. He is speaking of those very celestial intelligences who by the previous generation had been regarded as the revealers of the Divine will, the messengers from God

to man and the ambassadors from man to God.
Just in proportion as Christianity has widened and
deepened his sense of the Divine nature, the soul of
the apostle feels fretted by the intervention of lesser
natures between himself and the Divine. It is an
impulse of protestantism that impels him. It is the
struggle of his personality to be in contact with the
apex of the universe, the craving of his nature to be
at one with the Infinite Essence of all things. He
feels that the belief in principalities and powers is
practically the belief in a prison-house. In the old
days, when his God was an isolated unit, he had
welcomed them as imaginary steps up the steep
ascent which divided him from the summit of creation. But now that he had believed in Christ they
were simply hindrances, impediments, barriers, middle walls of partition between his eyes and the
light of heaven. Instead of being the steps on
which he could rise, they were the stones on which
he must stumble, the obstacles which blocked his
way in running the race which was set before him ;
and he felt irresistibly that, until he had cleared
them out of his path, he was in the presence of
an element which might separate him from the
love of God.

But as Paul enters on the period of his captivity
his language on this subject becomes much more
triumphant. When he wrote to the Romans his
triumph was still in the future, something which he

expected in the light of faith. But when he wrote
to the Ephesians and Colossians the victory was no
longer a matter of faith but of sight; the principalities and powers of the heavenly places were already
vanquished. They were vanquished by being superseded, by having their province taken away through
the service rendered by a Higher Life. Christ had
conquered them by passing beyond them, and he
had passed beyond them by stooping beneath them.
They had been devised to meet a supposed emergency which was not a real emergency. The Divine
Life had been thought incapable of uniting with the
sufferings of the human life because the union with
such suffering implied a union with sin. But now
the Divine Life itself had solved the enigma; it had
united itself even with sin. It had come down not
only through the intervening chasm between itself
and the celestial spirits, but through all that subsequent region which the celestial spirits had been
supposed to traverse. It had founded a new ideal
of empire, an ideal in which greatness ceased to
be identified with unapproachableness, and became
synonymous with its opposite. It had established a
new order of dominion, a dominion in which to be
king of the universe was to be the head of a body,
and therefore the servant of all its members. It
had revealed a new type of majesty, a type in which
the essence of regal glory was not to be a solitary
unit deriving its distinction from its distinctiveness,

but to be the burden-bearer of all life, the supporter
of all weakness, the recipient of all sorrow. The
universe of Paul had passed through a transformation analogous to that which his own life had passed
through.   It had been transformed like himself
from a Jewish into a Christian existence, from a
life whose glory was isolation into a life whose joy
was fellowship. It had broken down its middle wall
of partition between its centre and its apex, and
had displayed to the eye of the beholder a line of
uninterrupted communion between the highest and
the lowest.

It would not be difficult from the epistles of the
captivity to give many illustrations of this sense of
emancipation with which Paul beheld the disappear-
ance of the celestial mediators ; but we shall content
ourselves with one. Speaking of Christ as having
by death and resurrection united the extremes of
universal being, Paul says, " Having put off from
Himself the principalities and the powers, He made
a show of them openly, triumphing over them." [1]
What are these principalities and powers which
Christ is said to have abolished ? Are they that
hierarchy of angelic spirits who are called the ministers to the heirs of salvation ?   Are they that company of malign intelligences that are supposed to
constitute the army of the Prince of the air ? They

[1] Col. ii. 15.

are neither. They are not actual existences but existences in the imagination. The imagination was all along the sphere of their action and the source of their hurtfulness. Their evil lay in the fact that they did not represent the universe as it really was, but the universe as it was not. They were the attempt to supply a non-existent emergency, a difficulty that was only seeming. They were devised to fill up a chasm in the universe which existed only in fancy. They were intended to connect the centre with the apex, in ignorance of the fact that the centre was connected with the apex already. They owed their being to the supposition that the Divine Life was bound to be a life of solitude, whereas of all lives it was bound to be the least alone. Christianity had broken the illusion. It had revealed the paradox that the greatest is of necessity the least, that the height of imperialism is the depth of service. Paul's is a protest against the dividing of the universe,—a protest against the later Judaism, against the earlier Gnosticism, against all of every creed and soil who, by the interposition of principalities and powers, had denied the uniting bond which connects the highest with the lowest. He did for the first century what the man of modern science has done for the nineteenth—proclaimed the unity of nature and the binding of all things under a common law. The only difference between the man of modern

R

science and the founder of Christian theology is this, that while the one finds his principle of unity in believing in a force which he cannot define, the other has discovered it by taking one additional step—by assigning to that force the attribute of personality and calling it by the name of Love.

CHAPTER XII.

PAUL AND THE FAMILY.

A MAN'S theory of the universe is the key-note to his estimate of family relations. Whatever he has conceived to be the order of universal life becomes to him the pattern and model after which he would like to frame the circle of his own home. It was impossible that Paul could have passed through the development indicated in the previous chapter without experiencing an essential change in his attitude towards everyday life. It was inevitable that the new view which Christianity had given him of the universe should transform his old view of the family and the home. We have seen that his Christian conception of the universe had been a direct revolt from his Jewish conception; I now go on to show that his Christian conception of the family was also a direct revolt from that conception of the family which was entertained by his nation.

The highest ideal of the Jewish mind was kinghood. It was an ideal which had its beginning in the sphere of religion ; it did not ascend from earth to heaven but it descended from heaven to earth. The Jew's first admiration of kinghood was derived from the contemplation of the universe. He looked upon the face of nature and beheld there the impress of power. The objects which excited his wonder, the objects which stimulated his inspiration, were the physical forces which manifest themselves in dynamical strength. His very first conception of Divine action in the universe was the conception of a rushing mighty wind moving on the face of the waters,[1] and bearing down all opposition to its will. From this time forth the attribute which, above all others, he beheld in Deity was power. When he thought of God he thought of Him as, beyond every-thing else, a king. If he placed Him in solitary majesty, he did so in vindication of His kinghood. He wanted to think of Him as the Absolute Ruler, and, to assist that thought, he refused to allow Him any second in command ; he placed Him apart from all other intelligences that he might express the fact of His regal independence. The watchword of his whole theological system was " the kingdom of God."

Now this was the thought which in the history of the Jewish nation was brought down from heaven to earth. It was impossible it should exist in the air without in time descending to the plain, impossible

[1] Gen. i. 2.

it should be an article of theology without becoming also an article of social morals. That ideal of empire which the Jew saw in the heavens he began ere long to see on the earth. It was inevitable that he should fashion the things on the plain after the pattern of the things on the mount. Accordingly, it is not long before we find him transferring his ideas of Divine sovereignty into the sphere of everyday life. The central sphere of his everyday life was the home circle. It was here, therefore, that the Jew first transplanted that ideal of imperialism which he had found in the outward universe. The Old Testament tells us in so many words that the Hebrew's ideal of the home circle was modelled after the pattern of what he had seen in physical nature. Abraham stands below the stars and is impressed with their vastness and their innumerableness, and the vision suggests to him the possibility of founding a family which should represent in its numbers and its ramifications this exhaustless spectacle of the heavens. "So shall thy seed be," is the ideal of family life which floats before his mind—an ideal whose essence is imperialism and whose glory is the acquisition of power. From the days of Abraham onward, the home circle becomes to the Jew the central image of that sovereignty which he had seen mirrored in the heavens. Forbidden to make any graven image of the Divine power, he substituted one which was not graven. He took the family as the representative in miniature of that form of empire which he had figured in the universe. The two ideas for which the family lived were multiplication and ramification. The life of the individual had little personal significance; it was but a tributary to the family life. The very thought of personal immortality was held in abeyance. The immortality which was flashed before the eyes of the individual soul was the perpetuated life of the nation through the growth and expansion of the family life. Hence the agency which above all others was recognised and valued was marriage. I do not know of any incident of the Old Testament more significant than the story of Jephthah's daughter. That a father should sacrifice the life of his child in obedience to a religious vow is itself startling enough, but we are more startled still to be told that the main source of the lamentation was the fact of the maiden's virginity. Yet the picture is true to the life of the nation. The individual existed only for the sake of the matrimonial tie, and the matrimonial tie existed only for the sake of posterity. That one should become a thousand, that the unit should expand into the multitude, was the object for which every life was born and the goal to which every life aspired.

And the result was one of the greatest disasters which can befall any nation—the depression and degradation of womanhood. I say depression and

degradation, because there is evidence that the spirit
of the Hebrew race was originally turned in an
opposite direction. The earlier books of the Old
Testament give ample indication that the original
ideal of womanhood was higher than the subsequent
ideal. The paradisiac state was figured as a state
in which the sexes were of equal dignity, in which
the woman was bone of the man's bone and flesh of
the man's flesh. The first years of the people's
history exhibit an occasional respect for woman
which can only be accounted for as the survival of
an earlier culture. Sarah triumphs in the house of
Abraham ; Rebekah is unrivalled in the house of
Isaac ; Rachel and Leah, notwithstanding the broken
monogamy, preserve the home features in the house
of Jacob ; Miriam sings in the desert, and Deborah
leads the van on the other side of Jordan. Yet, all
the time, the cloud is deepening, and the cloud is the
worship of physical power. As the hope of empire
draws nearer, as the tribe begins to expand into a
nation and the nation begins to realise its definite
destiny, the utilitarian value of marriage extinguishes
its sacramental value, and woman, just in proportion
as she absorbs attention in the sphere of numerical
development, becomes a nonentity and a cipher in
every other sphere.

By-and-by the national dream is broken. There
comes a period of great depression in which the glory
of the kingdom passes away and the hope of numeri-

cal greatness perishes; it is the age of the captivity. Yet, just as the old hope expires, a new hope appears. As Judea loses the prospect of reaching imperial greatness through the multiplication of her people she receives the prospect of becoming great through the appearance of a single man. The expectation that from the lineage of David there should arise a great political ruler to restore the fortunes of Israel did not begin with the captivity; but the captivity made it to every man a possible object of ambition to become the parent of such a king. As long as the line of David was visibly distinguishable from other lines that ambition was limited to royalty. But when the storm came that laid the nation low, it tore off the branches of the Davidic tree and scattered them far and wide. It made them indistinguishable from the branches of other trees; it levelled them with the life of the common dust. And by that very act it widened their influence. Hitherto, the hope of being an ancestor of the political Messiah could only be shared by the royal house; but, when the branches of the royal house became untraceable, that hope became possible to all. Who could tell at what moment he might be brought into family relationship with the root of Jesse? Who could tell what matrimonial connection might in an instant unite him with that tree of national life from which prophets had predicted that the mighty branch should come? And so, at the very moment when the fortunes of

Israel were most depressed, nay, by the very reason
of their extreme depression, the utilitarian value of
the marriage state acquired a new significance and
a fresh power. I cannot say that, so far as the
domestic altar was concerned, the new attractive
force was one whit more salutary than the old. In
the new, as in the old, the woman was simply a piece
of mechanism set up to work out a political end.
She was merely an instrument of state machinery
designed to achieve a purpose external to her own
destiny. She was an agency to accelerate the coming of a kingdom which, when it did come, would be
foreign to her mission and alien to her capacity—
a kingdom whose force was physical, whose strength
was corporeal, whose aim was drastic, and whose
method was crushing. She was appointed to spin
a web by whose completion she must die.

I have dwelt at some length on this feature of
Jewish home life because it may help to explain a
matter in Paul's Christian attitude on which there
has been frequent misapprehension. When Paul
embraced Christianity he passed out of sympathy
with the family life of his nation. His departure,
indeed, from the national ideal of the family is the
earliest moral feature of his separation from Judaism.
No one can read the seventh chapter of 1st Corinthians without being impressed with the fact that
his attitude towards marriage was at that time, to
say the least, non-sympathetic. The most he could

say in its advocacy was to regard it as a shield
against possible evils which might arise in its absence. But there has been considerable misconcep-
tion as to the motive of Paul's coldness in this
matter. For one thing, it has been frequently
averred that his want of sympathy for the marriage
state originated in his general depreciation of womanhood. A more ungrounded assertion is not to be
conceived. One of the most distinctive elements in
Paul's Christian experience was the recognition of
the claims of woman ; in nothing is he more sharply
distinguished from his Jewish countrymen. Even
those passages in which he seems to depreciate
are dictated by a precisely opposite motive—the
desire to conserve for woman that distinctive and
peculiar sphere of which Jewish politics had deprived her. When he deprecates the notion that
a woman should teach in the public assemblies,[1] he
does so on the ground that teaching in the public
assemblies is not her sphere but inimical to her
sphere. The sphere which he desires to conserve
for her, or rather to create for her, is ministration.
He looks upon it as her true province, nay, as her
true power, to be a helper rather than an originator.
The origination of action belongs in his view to the
man ; the reception and transmission of action is the
gift of the woman. What else than this does he
mean when he says, "For this cause ought the

[1] 1 Cor. xiv. 34, 35.

woman to have power on her head because of the angels"?[1] The power on the head is of course a veil; but the very expression lifts the symbol into a thought. That which to the man would be a covering is to the woman declared to be a power. Her capacity of stooping to the will of others, her susceptibility of bending to the needs of those around her, if it separates her sharply from the man, is said to ally her with a greater than the man—the angel. To Paul, as to the writer of the epistle to the Hebrews, the name of angel is synonymous with that of ministering spirit. In linking the mission of the woman with the mission of the angel he is paying her the highest of all compliments, and he is paying her the compliment in that very direction in which she had been contemned. Her veil is declared to be her power. The ministrant element which Judaism had suppressed is to be made by Christianity her glory. Christianity is to Paul above all things a feminine strength. Its masculine features are recognised as mutable and perishable: prophecies were to fail, tongues were to cease, knowledge was to vanish away; but the strength that seeketh not her own, that suffereth long and is kind, that is not easily provoked, that vaunteth not herself, that beareth, believeth, hopeth and endureth all things, this was to be the permanent essence, the abiding power of the new evangel.[2]

[1] 1 Cor. xi. 10.　　　　[2] 1 Cor. xiii.

We cannot, then, account for Paul's neutral attitude towards the married state by any theory of his depreciation of womanhood. We are bound to recognise the fact that his neutral attitude exists side by side with a recognition of the claims of woman which had not been made for centuries. There is another ground to which we are unable to refer Paul's coldness towards the matrimonial state. It is sometimes said that he was influenced in this direction by the belief that it was one of the things which Christ's second coming would dissolve. Why, then, on the same principle does he not advise the discontinuance of the Lord's Supper? Nothing can be more certain than that he regarded the Lord's Supper as a provisional institution destined to pass away. Why, then, does he not speak of this institution in the form in which he speaks of marriage—as something which may be conveniently disregarded by those who have reached a larger light? He certainly does not so speak of it. He looks upon it as an ordinance which must last as long as the world lasts, which can only end when the dawn has already melted into the day. It is to be an institution in whose observance there is to be no break, in whose continuity there is to be no pause, in whose solemnity there is to be no suspension, until the shadow shall dissolve into the substance and the type shall be lost in its fulfilment, "as often as ye eat this bread, ye do show the Lord's death till

He come." [1] What is that difference between these two cases which has necessitated on the part of the apostle such opposite modes of treatment?

In the answer to this question lies the solution of the whole problem. And the answer is not far to seek. The Lord's Supper, fleeting as it was conceived to be, was still in Paul's sight a sacrament; the ordinance of marriage, as Paul had hitherto known it, was not a sacrament. Remember where he had come from—from the camp of the Philistines. Remember what in that camp the matrimonial tie had been—a bond of purely utilitarian value connecting human souls on the ground of expediency and uniting them for purposes extraneous to the domestic life. Remember, above all, that on the mind of the apostle there had not yet broken the full sweep of the sacramental light. He had not yet awakened to the truth of Christ's secular priesthood. He had not yet realised the fact that there was an outer as well as an inner membership in the body of Christ, and that He could not be the sacrificial head of the Church without being the sacrificial head of the world too. He was still waiting for that final revelation which only came to him in the Roman captivity—the revelation that the secular sphere mirrored everywhere the law of the sacred, and that the symbol of the Lord's Supper in the Church was reflected on the waters of outward life. Secular and sacred

[1] 1 Cor. xi. 26.

were as yet two spheres to him, and between heaven
and earth there ran a line of the sharpest separation.
Is it surprising that in this middle period of his
history—the period in which Divine grace stood out
in bold antithesis to the existing life of nature, he
should have looked with a feeling akin to coldness
upon an institution whose only recognised function
had hitherto been the perpetuation of that life ?

But now the scene changes. We pass over a brief
period of five years, and we are ushered into a new
world of Paul's experience. The transition from
Corinth into Rome is to him more than the transition from freedom into bondage; it is the passage
from partialness into fulness of view. His vision of
Divine truth at Corinth had partaken somewhat of
the manner of Greece. Just as the Greek beheld the
Divine influence only where he beheld the human
beauty, so Paul in the Corinthian stage of his history
had recognised the sacramental headship only where
he saw the union of the ecclesiastical members. But
when Paul reached Rome he began to see after the
manner of Rome. The kingdom of God to him took
that form which the kingdom of Cæsar assumed to
the Latin race—the form of a membership which
was connected with all other memberships. As the
image of the heavenly sunshine glitters in the earthly stream, even so in the institutions of the Roman
empire did Paul behold a possible reflection of the
sacrificial priesthood of Christ. I say, " a possible

reflection." The institutions of that empire were very far from exhibiting actually any such spectacle. Nevertheless, the moment that to the eye of Paul the world of time revealed itself as the possible mirror of eternity, the world of time in his eyes became sanctified, glorified. Its possibility became to him its only reality. Its present reality was a fiction, an illusion, a dream. That for which it lived was its golden future, and in the light of that future its value was to be measured. To Paul in the Roman dungeon the secular world shone with an ideal light. What the citizens of the empire beheld merely as a coin bearing the superscription of Cæsar was reflected to his gaze with the stamp and impress of the Son of man. Instead of contemplating, as in days of yore, the dissolution of its life, he began to contemplate the Christianising of its life. Every form, every institution, became in his sight consecrated to a coming baptism—a baptism in which the membership of the Lord's Supper was to become the type and symbol after whose pattern all other memberships were to be modelled, and in whose sacred likeness all secular things were to appear.

Amongst those secular things which Paul saw transfigured in the light of Christ, stood in the foremost rank the relations of the family circle. Next to the big universe of nature came to his sight the little world of home. We have seen in the previous chapter how, in the thought of Christ's secular headship the universe of nature was transformed; we are now to see how in the same thought the idea of marriage became transfigured. That it did pass through such a transfiguration it seems to me impossible to deny. Let any man read the seventh chapter of 1st Corinthians, and turn afterwards to the later epistles, he will, I am convinced, be impressed with the thought that in relation to the ordinance of marriage he is in a different atmosphere. It is not merely that in these later epistles the apostle has ceased to warn mankind of matrimonial dangers; this would be simply an argument from silence, which is the most inconclusive of all arguments. But the point which impresses me in these epistles is not so much the change in adverse criticism as the change in the mode of commendation. He had all along maintained the lawfulness of the matrimonial state; he had in certain cases asserted its expediency. But at the stage of the Roman captivity marriage has become to him not only in some cases expedient, but in every case sacramental. Its negative merit has been exchanged for a positive glory. It had all along the virtue of a shield to ward off greater dangers; it is now invested with a virtue on its own account. It has become in Paul's sight the shadow and the type on earth of that which he regarded as the central fact of heaven—the union between the Christ of love and the Church which He had purchased with His blood.

Take in illustration that passage which has become typical of the Pauline view of marriage and authoritative as the rule of Christian observance—Ephesians v. 22 and sequel. When we read the opening words, " Wives, submit yourselves unto your own husbands, as unto the Lord," our first impression is that we are only listening to one of the many assertions by which Eastern despotism proclaims the authority of the male over the female. But, as we read on, our view is entirely altered. We find that the meaning given to the word submission is no longer Eastern nor even Roman. When we are told that the husband is the head of the wife, " even as Christ is the head of the Church and the saviour of the body," we are confronted not by an intensification but by a limitation of marital authority. Remember what to Paul the headship of Christ is ; it is in the most literal sense the saving of the body. It is a reign no doubt over the members, but it is not a reign after the analogy of kinghood. It is in its deepest essence a priesthood of suffering. It is a mastership over the members which is reached by taking their pains, a pre-eminence which is achieved by accepting the lowest room. It is this and nothing else than this that Paul recognises as the ideal type of marital authority. He offers it to the Gentile world as the extreme opposite of Eastern despotism. Preserving in words the ancient relation, it is yet in reality the

reversal of that relation. As long as the husband
was the king, the life of the wife was subservient to
his own; but when he became the head, his own life
became subservient. That this is Paul's view, it
is from the passage before us impossible to doubt.
" Husbands, love your wives," he says, " even as Christ
also loved the Church, and gave Himself for it."
For almost the first time in the history of the world
the man in the matrimonial contract stands forth as
the sacrificial party—sacrificial by reason of his manhood, subservient on account of his headship. He is
to the members of the household what Christ is to
the members of the Church—the centre of all the
nerves and therefore the bearer of all the pain. I
say, " *almost* for the first time," for here again Paul
preserves his conservatism even amidst his progress;
he claims to have a foothold in the past. As he had
reached his conception of faith by going back beyond
Judaism, he reaches his conception of marriage by
going back beyond Hebraism. His eye rests on the
picture of that primeval paradise where the nuptial
torch of sacrifice was originally carried by the male,
where it was not the woman that left father and
mother to cleave unto the man, but the man who
left father and mother to cleave unto his wife.[1] He
feels that if woman was to be exalted, emancipated,
delivered from her life of bondage, it could only be

[1] Eph. v. 31.

by transforming the ideal of the husband into her own likeness, by making manhood itself a feminine power, by transferring to the function of empire that thought of ministration which had hitherto been regarded as the badge of the slave.

And truly Paul was right; the facts of the future have confirmed and justified his view. The history of modern times as distinguished from ancient times is the history of domestic life as distinguished from merely national life. The greatest gift of Christianity to the social fabric is the development of the idea of home. Here, for the first time, the life of the family stands forth without reference to political institutions, and for its own sake alone. Here, for the first time, the refinements and amenities of the domestic altar are cultivated for no utilitarian object, but simply for appreciation of their own beauty and joy.[1] Every step of this development is contemporaneous with the steps of that progress by which the woman rises in the social scale. Just in proportion as she becomes an authority in the family circle does the family circle itself become a centre of national life. The Roman empire did not pass away until it had taken the initiative in transferring the education of the child from the hands of the father into the

---

[1] Even the fifth commandment is based upon a political ground, and is besides one-sided; contrast the reciprocal relation in Col. iii. 20, 21.

hands of the mother. The process was long and
devious but it has been worth the pains; it has
imposed upon the Western world that influence of
female culture which the Zenana Mission seeks to
impose upon the East. Yet, if we ask what has
been the ultimate source of this refinement in the
idea of home, we shall be obliged to confess that the
amelioration of woman herself has been rather an
effect than a cause. We shall be compelled to recognise the fact that the change has its root in a more
radical movement still—a movement which transformed not the female but the male, and which
exerted its earliest influence rather on the husband
than on the wife. We shall find that Paul has
himself struck the key-note of the new evangel by
placing the Christianised glory of marriage in the
transformation effected on the very idea of empire.
In recognising the truth that in the new *régime* the
husband is head of the wife, "as Christ is head of
the Church," he has put his hand upon the real
source of that refining influence which has produced the elevation of woman and created the
atmosphere of home. He has directed attention to
the fact that Christianity has planted a feminine
influence in the family circle mainly because it is
itself a feminine power, has changed the position of
the woman by altering the character of the man.
He has revealed as the ultimate ground of this mod-

ern development that change in the idea of dominion which has substituted the head of a body for the king of a state and has identified the rod of empire with the badge of service. In proclaiming Christ as the ideal of imperial as well as of ecclesiastical power he has himself been the pioneer of that civili- sation which is essentially modern and distinctively Christian.

CHAPTER XIII.

PAUL AND SOCIAL GRADATIONS.

WE have been tracing the development of Paul in its descent from heaven to earth. We have been trying to mark those successive steps by which he came down from the sacred into the secular. We have seen that his beginning, unlike the beginning of the other disciples, was in the heights of the upper air. We have seen that the course of his progress was exactly the antithesis of theirs; that, instead of rising from the ground to the skies, he had to descend from the skies to the ground. We have endeavoured to mark the stages of this progress from the solitudes of the Arabian desert to the chains of the Roman captivity. We have seen how Paul's interest in secular life was first awakened by the conviction that the headship of Christ over the Church was intended to be the symbol of all imperialism. We have seen how in that thought the secular world began to be transfigured to his sight. We have marked how first of all it changed to him the aspect of the universe and transformed his view of the nature of Divine government. We have observed next how his altered vision of the universe of nature began to reflect itself in the little empire of the family circle, how the redemption of the outer world was followed by the redemption of home. One sphere still remained—a sphere occupying a yet lower grade, a sphere which, more than all others, had mirrored the despotism of the old *régime;* I mean the relation of master and servant. It was inevitable that sooner or later Paul in the light of Christianity should be called to face this problem. The occurrence of a comparatively trivial circumstance precipitated the encounter. Nearly at the close of the first Roman captivity there befell a chance, or a providence, which brought the apostle of the Gentiles face to face with that great question which has been ever since the burning question of the social world—the reconciliation of man's ideal dignity with his position of servitude in a scene of toil.

Reading a little between the lines, it does not seem difficult to reconstruct the elements of the story. The earliest converts to Christianity had been generally made from the poorest class, but there were some notable exceptions. Amongst these was a wealthy citizen of Colossæ named Philemon. He had perhaps been brought under Paul's influence during the apostle's residence at

Ephesus. At all events he *was* brought under his influence and made by him a convert to the new faith. Like the centurion in the Gospel, he was a man of authority, having retainers or household slaves to whom he said "go" and "come." He seems, however, to have recognised even for them a right of personal freedom in the highest sphere. Himself a convert to Christianity, he did not force his retainers to become converts. He appears to have felt that there was in the human soul, even in the soul of a slave, a region which should be held sacred to the liberty of the individual will. He probably commanded his servants to be present at the hours of worship when the apostle happened to officiate in his house. He felt it to be his duty to give his retainers an opportunity of choice between the old faith and the new; but at this point he suspended his authority and left the choice itself to their own decision.

Amongst those household retainers was a youth named Onesimus. He was in the position I have indicated of having had the alternative placed before him between the setting and the rising sun. He had listened to Paul's expositions of the new faith. Intellectually and spiritually he was not convinced, but personally he was attracted. There was something about it which appealed specially and sooth- ingly to his own abject circumstances. That which enlisted his attention was its negative side—the side in which it stood forth as the opponent of man's bondage. As he heard those words of fire in which the apostle poured forth his denunciations against those who would trammel the rights of man, as he listened to those exhortations in which he called upon his auditors to stand fast in that liberty wherewith Christ had made them free, as there fell upon his ear those triumphant notes in which the new evangel proclaimed that where the Spirit of God was there was freedom, it seemed to him as if already the day of his emancipation had dawned. The theory of Christian liberty was as yet too subtle for him, but the fact was patent and inspiring. Here was a religion which asserted in the most unqualified terms the equality of all men before God, which declared in the most uncompromising accents that with Him there was no respect of persons, which maintained that in His sight all distinction was abolished between Jew and Gentile, Greek and barbarian, freeman and slave. Is it surprising that such a message should have sounded in his ears like strains of sweetest music? Is it wonderful that these negative notes of Christianity should have come to him like the tinkling of fairy bells repeating ever the one refrain, 'Come and be free'?

Time passed, and Paul departed for Jerusalem and for Rome. But absence does not melt the influence of that which once has had dominion over us. A great modern writer has said that the love of the heart for an object grows as much when it is separated from that object as when it dwells in its presence. So was it with Onesimus in his incipient attraction towards Christianity. Long after the voice of the preacher was withdrawn, its echoes remained in his ear uttering the old refrain of freedom. He had received for the first time a sense of the inherent dignity of man, of the dignity which belonged to a human soul irrespective of caste or circumstances. It did not occur to him that this very fact made it impossible for caste or circumstances to derogate from his dignity; that was a truth which he could only learn when he had exchanged the negative for the positive side of the Christian faith. Meantime he was still a pagan in heart, with a pagan's ideal of greatness. All that he had yet learned from Christianity was his right as a man to the essential privilege of manhood. He did not yet know that the essential privilege of manhood is not freedom but service, and that freedom is only valuable as the threshold to a voluntary service. And so, he chafed at the chain of whose binding he had been hitherto unconscious. That which was once tolerable to him became intolerable. The actual grievances of his position were exaggerated, imaginary grievances were added, and real compensations were ignored. The two ideas, of his own bondage and Christianity's promised emancipation, took joint possession of his heart and brain, until at last his place in the house of Philemon became to him as unbearable as if he had been the object of despotic tyranny.

One day, near the conclusion of Paul's first Roman period, the apostle was surprised by an apparition in the flesh of the slave Onesimus. He had fled from his master Philemon, and he came to justify his action by throwing himself into the arms of Paul and of the new religion. His meeting with the apostle must have been private, because the secret which he had to divulge would have been no secret in the presence of a Roman soldier. This proves, even if other evidence were not forthcoming,[1] that the restraint of Paul's first captivity had been latterly much mitigated. Onesimus communicated to the apostle the fact of his flight from the house of Philemon. It never occurred to him, it would never have occurred to any spectator, either Christian or pagan, that Paul would have done anything else than approve. The course taken by Onesimus appeared to be simply a following out of that which lay within the spirit of Christianity. Yet, to the astonishment of the spectators in every age, Paul's feeling was exactly the opposite. Instead of commending the step of Onesimus as one in accordance with the Christian spirit, he proceeds to reveal to Onesimus that the Christian spirit in his case had pointed in precisely the contrary direction. He shows him the

---

[1] No man who had not virtually been already acquitted would have written Philemon 22.

positive side of Christianity as a thing hitherto unknown to him, makes him an actual convert to the
new faith, and then sends him back to his master,
accompanied by one of the most courteous, high-
toned, and large-hearted letters which have ever been
addressed by man to man.

The question is, why? What is there in this
transaction that has surprised the spectator in every
age? It is not the feeling that Paul has done any
wrong to Onesimus. When we say that he sent him
back we merely describe the transaction as it appears
to the eye. Strictly speaking, Onesimus was not
sent back but went back. Nothing could be more
voluntary than his return to Philemon. All that
Paul did was to expel his old nature, to give him a
new will. The moment Onesimus became a Christian
it became impossible for him to see the matter in any
other light than that in which Paul saw it. This in
truth is the real mystery. We want to know why
Paul and Onesimus together did see the matter in
this light, why the fact of their Christianity impelled
them to make a concession to slavery. When England liberated her colonial slaves she liberated also
her colonial soil; if a slave thenceforth touched her
shores, he was by that act and in that instant free.
When Christianity proclaimed herself a land of freedom we should have expected a similar result. We
should have thought that, if a man fled from the
bonds of slavery and threw himself for protection at

the feet of a Christian apostle, his act would have been indorsed by that apostle as a preparation for the new evangel, and a sign of that coming freedom for which the human heart was longing.

We may be reminded that Paul was a Jew, and that as such it was natural that he should cherish the traditions of his country. But I must point out that Paul had emerged from the traditions of his country so far as they concerned the rights of man. He had conceived for himself a theory of human relations essentially different from that which had been embraced by his nation. His spiritual experience, as we have seen, had found its earliest stage in a vision of the future, its earliest hope in a second coming of the Son of man. Doubtless the picture was to him at first like the picture of the incipient creation in Genesis—without form and vague. But as time grew he filled it up, and by-and-by it became definite. When he had reached the stage of his Corinthian epistles there already floated before his mind the image of a glorious republic which should realise all the merits and eliminate all the defects of the ancient Messianic kingdom. It was a republic in which the idea of monarchy was to grow out of the idea of communism, in which there was to be a levelling down preparatory to a new gradation. The preliminary and initial phase was to be the abolition of present distinctions. There was to be a breaking down of the privileges of sex,

of the privileges of race, of the privileges of caste,—
an abolition of the pre-eminence of the male over
the female, of the Jew over the Gentile, of the
citizen over the servant.[1]   All men were to start
anew upon an equality, unfettered by the restric-
tions of the past, and unretarded by the distinctions
of birth or station.   Yet, this apparently commun-
istic arrangement had its source in an opposite
interest.   It was not designed to reduce men to one
level but to establish a new social grade.   Paul
knew well that, if society were made a plain to-day,
it would be studded again with mountains to-morrow.
He knew well that, however equal men might be in
rights, they were and would always be very unequal
in merits.   Accordingly, that state to which he looked
forward was not a democracy but an aristocracy;
only, it was an aristocracy in which the highest rank
was to be taken by the best man.   "Do you not
know," he cries, "that the saints shall judge the
world?"[2]   The survival of the fittest is to him a
matter of course, and the fittest are here not the
physically strongest but the morally purest.   God's
day of judgment is for him the time when every man
shall rise in his own order;[3] when every man shall
take his place in the social fabric not according to
his birth, not according to his nation, not according to
his clan, but according to his deed.[4]   Divine election

[1] Gal. iii. 28.   [2] 1 Cor. vi. 2.
[3] 1 Cor. xv. 23.   [4] 2 Cor. v. 10.

is to take the form of natural selection—a selection in which a man is to come to the front or to fall back into the rear irrespective altogether of whether he be freeman or slave, Gentile or Jew, but simply and entirely in proportion to the native strength that is in him, and on the ground of that suitability to the new environment which he has attained by the development of Christian experience.

It is true that for Paul all this was as yet in the future. It was not only in the future but in a future world. It had not occurred to him that the old and not a new environment might be the scene of his ideal government. In the Corinthian stage of his experience this world as a world was to him simply nil. It had not even reached the significance of being preparatory to a better state of things ; it existed as yet to his mind merely as an obstacle to the realisation of that state. The obstacle was one which must be removed by death. It had not yet broken on his mind that it might be removed by life—by the amelioration of the environment itself. Accordingly, in this Corinthian stage we are not surprised to find that he is by no means eager to stand forth as a social reformer. He is willing to let the institutions of the present world alone. He tells the slave to be obedient to his master, to abide in the situation wherein he is called, to regard with indifference the fact of his bondage. But he tells him at the same time the reason why. It is not because slavery is a thing indifferent, but because all the institutions of time are things fleeting and trans- itory. "The time is short," he says; "it remaineth that they that buy be as though they possessed not."[1] He sees that there is a period rapidly ap- proaching in which, for each individual soul, the distinction of bondman and freeman shall be seen to have been an illusion and a dream. The dissolution of the material chain to be effected by the hour of death shall prove that the bondman's chain was but one link in that great oppressive environment which has so long circumscribed the liberties of all man- kind. Seeing, therefore, that one common emanci- pation awaits both the bond and the free, it is not worth while for the bond to fret against their sepa- rate yoke; rather let them look upon it as only another incentive to the universal longing for the coming of that time when the fashion of this world shall pass away.

All this is perfectly intelligible and clearly logical. As long as a sharp line of separation exists between this world and other worlds, the only possibility of emancipation from present evils is that which lies through the gates of death. If Paul had written his epistle to Philemon at this stage, no one would have been surprised that he counselled Onesimus to return. But the epistle to Philemon was not written at this stage; it was the production of a later day.

[1] 1 Cor. vii. 29, 30.

It came not from the Corinthian but from the Ephesian and Colossian period. The transition from these periods was to Paul the transition into a new world—we might almost say, into the present world. When he stood in the streets of Rome there seemed to strike a new hour in the clock of time—the hour in which Christ for the first time became King of the secular world. The head of the Christian Church was recognised in a moment to be the head of all principalities and powers. The sharp line of separation which had divided this world from other worlds melted into thin air, and that Divine government which had hitherto been viewed exclusively in its heavenly relations was seen to exist for the sake of the common earth. Slavery could no longer be allowed to rest on the ground that the things of time were indifferent. The things of time had ceased to be indifferent; every secular object had become susceptible of a sacramental relation. Not only had Onesimus a right to freedom, but he had a right to freedom as an inhabitant of the present world. It was not merely something which he was entitled to claim in the sphere of religion; he was entitled to claim it in the sphere of human citizenship, to claim it on the ground of being a man. Why, then, with these changed premisses does Paul still retain the old conclusion? If Onesimus has a right to be free, and if freedom in the present world is no longer a thing indifferent, why does he induce him to return into a

T

surmounted slavery ? Why does he not exhort him
to claim with his Christian profession that right
which he regards as Christianity's inalienable privilege—the right of a free soul to follow the dictates
of its will?

It is because he feels that the main distinction of
Christianity is the power to sacrifice its rights. He
feels that, although Christianity professes to be the
life of the world, that profession is not its peculiarity ; it shares it with every religion under the sun.
Its peculiarity consists precisely in its power to *lay
down* its life, in its consent for the sake of the world
to take less than its due. Whenever Christ was
realised to be the head of all principalities and
powers Paul knew from that moment that the sacred
must bend to the secular. If the barren fig-tree was
to get a chance at all, it must meantime be preserved
even in its barrenness. The lofty ideal of Christianity must consent to pause, must postpone the realisation of that which was the end of its being. Just as
the headship of Christ in the religious world found
its immediate manifestation in bearing with the
imperfections of the bodily members, so the headship of Christ in the secular world must find its
immediate manifestation in bearing with the imperfections of existing things. It is in the light
of such a thought that one comes to understand that
strange conjunction of attributes by which a Christian writer, almost contemporaneous with Paul's

epistle to Philemon, has ventured to describe the
nature of the new dominion as " the kingdom and
patience of Christ." [1]

Let us apply this principle to the case before us.
Christianity had a right to proclaim the freedom of
man as man. Nothing was simpler than to make
such a proclamation. Paul had only to connive at
the flight of Onesimus and to indorse the act by his
own imprimatur; it would have been a signal to the
whole slave population of the world that the watchword of the new religion was emancipation from
servile bonds. What would have been the effect of
such a signal? Doubtless it would have instantaneously added to the numerical strength of Christianity;
the kingdom of heaven would immediately have been
taken by violence. And so would the kingdoms of
earth. It is impossible to conceive a more perfect
picture of anarchy than would have been created by
a sudden and successful insurrection of the slave
population. The numerical proportion of the bound
to the unbound in the Roman empire is a matter
of dispute, probably the bond outnumbered the free.
Figure anything approaching to such a proportion,
and then to the quantity add the quality. Consider
that the slave population represented at its worst
that state which we designate by the name of Paganism—a name which embraces as its leading characteristic the predominance of the sensuous over the

[1] Rev. i. 9.

spiritual. It was paganism without its restraints and
without its refinements. What would have been
the effect of the emancipation of these millions—
the emancipation of an un-Christianised, unhuman-
ised horde impelled by the fanaticism of a new
watchword, accomplished in a moment of time and
achieved by a stroke of violence ? Could it have
had any other result than one—the transformation
of order into anarchy, the uprooting of that line of
civilisation on which Christianity itself had begun
to move ?

That such a thought passed through Paul's mind
is perfectly manifest from the second epistle to the
Thessalonians. So far back as that early writing we
find the mind of the apostle perturbed by the spectacle of incipient lawlessness in the Roman empire.
Beneath the calm surface he feels that there is brood-
ing a storm. He is conscious that there are underground forces whose action is only restrained by the
powers at the summit, and which, if these powers
were removed, would sweep relentlessly over the
whole system of law and order. He is not thinking
simply of the slave population, but of the masses in
general. " Even now," he says, " the spirit of lawlessness works secretly, only, he that hindereth will hin-
der until he be taken out of the way." [1] " He that
hindereth " is clearly the Roman emperor. The reference is meant to be complimentary. Cæsar was

[1] 2 Thess. ii. 7.

not Paul's hero, and the Roman government was not
Paul's ideal, but he felt that in relation to existing
evils both had a remedial mission to perform. He
felt that the iron hand of that imperial constitution,
however oppressive it might be in its intrinsic nature,
was yet achieving a work which no other hand could
have achieved. It was keeping down from the surface
forces of the most fiery and insubordinate character,
forces which had long been burning underground
and which only waited an opportunity to make their
eruption into the upper air. That sooner or later
they would obtain their object Paul had no doubt;
he felt that eventually the restraining power of the
empire would be taken out of the way. Yet it was
to him no matter of congratulation. He stood
appalled before the picture which his own imagination had created — the picture of a subterranean
anarchy let loose by the removal of the world's outer
crust. And if Paul feared this even in those days
when he wrote to the Thessalonians—days of ascetic
reaction from the present order of things—is it likely
that he would have feared it less in that period of
reconciliation with the present when he wrote the
epistle to Philemon? Is it not patent that the same
dread of anarchy which had impelled him in the
past to deprecate the loosening of the Roman hand,
was now impelling him to deprecate any sudden and
violent liberation even from that physical slavery
which was contrary to the spirit of the new religion?

It may be asked, Was not Onesimus after his conversion fit for freedom? Undoubtedly he was, and probably a few hundreds besides. But it was just here that in the view of Paul the Christian principle manifested its most distinctive power. It was of the essence of Christianity that one should die for the people, that the few should give their life as a ransom for the many. The headship of Christ was itself based upon the idea of a membership in which the pains of the whole body were concentrated in a single organ. Could there be a grander occasion for the illustration of this principle than that which had now presented itself? Onesimus had set himself free; he was fit for freedom, and in the sight of God he had a right to freedom. But the vast majority of his class were utterly unfit for such liberation. What if they should do what Onesimus had done—emancipate themselves by an act of rebellion? And how was such a catastrophe to be averted? Clearly by the sacrifice of Onesimus himself. If his conversion to Christianity were real, his first act as a Christian must be the renunciation of his own right; he must forego his crown and take up his ancient cross. The men of his own class were unripe for the emancipation he had himself attained; let him resign this emancipation. Let him offer himself as an oblation for his people. Let him voluntarily go back into that depressed position from which he had striven to be free. Let him de-

liberately go down again into that valley of humiliation from which it had been the aspiration of his life
to be exalted. So would the valley itself become to
him the mountain, and, in the sacrifice of that right
to liberty which as a Christian he had the power to
claim, he would reach a higher exhibition of the distinctive power of man.

I have tried to reproduce that state of mind which
probably dictated to Paul the singular course adopted
in the epistle to Philemon. I do not regard this
incident as simply a biographical episode in the
apostle's life. To me it is one of the most distinctly
marked stages in the development of his spiritual
experience. Nowhere in the course of Paul's history
has he hitherto displayed so much deference for the
secular institutions of the world. We stand here
upon that transition line which leads into the final
period of the apostle's life—a period which is at once
antithetical and complementary to the experience of
his earlier days. As we see before us the man of the
past and the man of the present—the man who wrote
the epistles to the Corinthians and the man who
wrote the epistle to Philemon, we feel that we have
passed to the opposite bank of the river. There is
no contradiction, there is no annulling of former
sentiments, yet there is a distinct development and
the occupation of a position from which the eye can
command a larger view. When he wrote his first
epistle to the Corinthians his mind was occupied

with the problem how much the secular ought to yield to the sacred; when he wrote his epistle to Philemon his mind was engrossed with the question how much the sacred ought to yield to the secular. Both were legitimate problems, both questions were answered in accordance with the Christian spirit, but both were not asked at the same time. The one was put in the days when Paul had just completed his spiritual struggle; the other was suggested in the days when the struggle had faded from his memory and the calm of mellow autumn had come. At the earlier stage he had been confronted by the question whether in their secular feasts the disciples of the new faith might eat the flesh which had been offered to an idol; he had himself no doubt whatever of the lawfulness, but he bowed before the common Christian conscience.[1] Here, in the latter stage, he bows before another tribunal—that of the common *heathen* conscience. A runaway slave appeals to him for freedom on the ground of that very religion whose pioneer he professed to be. The right to freedom was confessed and undoubted, but the needs of the Gentile world demanded that it should be postponed; Paul yielded to the Gentile need and in-spired the runaway to return.

Here is a change of standpoint, not amounting, indeed, to any alteration in principle, yet distinctly exhibiting the fact that Paul had passed over to

[1] 1 Cor. viii. 13.

another side of the truth. How are we to explain
the transition ? How can we better explain it than
by a recognition of that order of development
through which the apostle's life was gradually unfolded ? It was not that, as time advanced and as
the shadows of age deepened on his path, the ardour
of his early fire grew paler; it was rather that his
early fire took hold on new objects and extended the
range of its ardour. The secular had become to him
itself the sacred. The middle wall of partition which
so long had divided the kingdom of Christ from the
kingdoms of the world had in his sight been broken
down, and Christ was recognised not merely as the
head of a redeemed humanity but as the head of
principalities and powers still heathen. The Gentile
world, unknown to itself, had to Paul become a
theocracy—a government which, with all its imperfections, was ministering to the ends of the universe.
As such, its every institution was by him viewed
with reverence—a reverence not unlike to that which
he still cherished for the mission of the Jewish law;
and even the tare of slavery he would not suffer to
be plucked with violence, lest haply in gathering up
the tare men should root out also the wheat with it.

CHAPTER XIV.

THE COMPLETED JOURNEY.

I HAVE said that the epistle to Philemon forms the transition line into Paul's final period. That period embraces what are called the pastoral epistles—those to Timothy and Titus. The figure of the apostle which has been long hid from view within the walls of the prison-house suddenly and for a brief space emerges once more into the light, and resumes its missionary journeys. It is but a temporary return of the working day, and is followed ere long by a re-closing of the prison wall to be opened only by the hand of death. But, momentary as is the apparition, it is long enough to give us a glimpse of the man. What does that glimpse reveal? Is it the same Paul on whom our eyes rested previous to the first Roman captivity? We have seen the sun before it entered into the cloud; we have lost sight of it for a few hours, and now, almost on the borders of evening, it comes once more into view. Is the sun on the borders of evening the same as that which entered into the cloud? To drop the metaphor, is the Paul who writes the epistles to Timothy and Titus identical with the Paul who wrote the epistles to Galatia and Corinth?

Let us imagine for a moment that all the writings of Paul had been lost with the exception of the epistle to the Galatians and the three pastoral epistles. Let us suppose that when his figure was hid from the eye his voice also had been hid from the ear, and that during the whole time of his Roman captivity there had disappeared all record of his thoughts and actions. Let us conceive, therefore, that when he emerged from his captivity his friends had no other standard by which to compare him than the memory of those old days when they had seen him brandishing the sword against the false Judaisers; what would have been the conclusion to which they must have come? Would it not have been the great sense of contrast which was presented between the Paul of the present and the Paul of the past? Undoubtedly. For no man can read the pastoral epistles over against the epistle to the Galatians without perceiving that he is in the presence of a man in many respects changed. If one were asked to describe the main feature of the change, he would perhaps best express it by saying that in the pastoral epistles the warfare was out of him. In the Galatian letter he is brandishing the

sword. We there catch the figure of one who is
consciously in the heat of battle, who sees only two
sides of the question, and is persuaded that, on the
adoption of one or the other, life or death depends.
But in the pastoral letters there is no longer a trace
of battle. The sword has been put up into its scab-
bard. The fiery accents of the soldier have been replaced by the calm words of the old man, breathing
at every turn "Peace, peace." · There is everywhere
the deprecation of strife, everywhere the effort to
find a common ground between the two sides of the
question. Looking on this picture and on that, and
seeing no intermediate picture, one would naturally
be tempted to ask whether the glow of Christian
enthusiasm had not itself subsided, and whether the
diminution of early fire did not owe its origin to the
cessation of early zeal.

Such, I say, might have been our impression, had
we possessed no intermediate record between the
Galatian and the pastoral epistles. But we do possess such a record, and this makes all the difference.
We have a series of letters intervening between the
days of the fiery soldier and the days of the peaceful old man, and these do not only intervene between them — they connect them. They show us
that the change in the demeanour of Paul is the
result not of a diminished but of an expanded
energy. They reveal to us the fact that the production of this change has been itself the very plan

of development on which his life was all along designed to move. They tell us that the plan of this development was the descent of a mountain. When he wrote the epistle to the Galatians he was at the top of the mountain; when he wrote the pastoral epistles he was at the foot; his intermediate life was the passage between the extremes. The top of the mountain was the heavenly side. His spiritual history had begun with the vision of the resurrection Christ; the glory of the world to come had extinguished for a time the sense of this world's possible glory. It was the age in which the life of the spirit was naturally and very properly suspicious of all interference on the part of the flesh, suspicious even of the influence of those things which on the surface seemed to be indifferent. Yet clearly it was impossible, undesirable, that such isolation should be maintained. If Christianity was to be a life for the world, it must be a life *in* the world; it must conquer the mountain not by keeping at the top of it but by traversing its slopes. It was inevitable that, if Paul was to be a complete man, he must be able to take his stand on what now to him was the opposite side of the question. Accordingly, we expect to find, and we do find, that the course of his subsequent development is the history of a descending process, in which he is ever stepping further down from heaven to earth, and ever drawing nearer to the appropriation of that

secular field which had originally been the barrier
to the advance of the spiritual life.

The pastoral epistles are confessedly the completion of this descent. In the letter which he
wrote during his second captivity, he takes a retro-
spect of his whole career, and as the result of the
final view he declares that he had reached that
point of perfected ripeness which had been the
object of his journey.[1] " I have fought a good fight,
I have finished my course, I have kept the faith,"
are the words in which he sums up the history of
his spiritual experience. And certainly, if the order
of Paul's development has been such as we have described, these pastoral epistles furnish for his life a
consistent and appropriate close. If the progress
of his pilgrimage has been a descent from the sacred
to the secular, the climax of that progress has as-
suredly been reached here. Nowhere has the spirit
of Paul entered so thoroughly and so pronouncedly
into the sphere of secularism. If the first part of
his life was the period in which he was called to
defend the spirit against the encroachments of the
flesh, it might almost be said that this closing period
was the time in which he was called to defend the
flesh against the encroachments of the spirit. Standing at the foot of the mountain, he stands on the
basis of pure humanity and recognises the essential
sacredness of what once to him had been merely

[1] 2 Tim. iv. 6, 7.

mundane. The key-note of his life in this period is struck in the suggestive words "the man Christ Jesus."[1] Very singular is it that Paul's final gaze on Christ should have been distinctively and pre-eminently the gaze on His humanity. In the former days his eyes had centred chiefly on that which was Divine; he had begun with the vision of the Christ of resurrection, and for a time he could look on nothing but the resurrection light. Yet his ripest hour was to be that in which his eyes were to be transfixed by the vision of the man. The sight which came to him latest was the sight which had come to the other disciples earliest—the full revelation of the human Jesus, the completed view of the Christ of Nazareth. Therefore it is that in his final utterances he emphasises in the Messiah, above all things, the man. The resurrection light fades into the background and the image of human nature in its perfect form appears. And, because the image of human nature appears, humanity itself, and for its own sake, becomes the object of his solici-tude. Religion takes a wider sweep; the temple ex-pands to embrace the outer courts of the sanctuary. The interests of man as man rise to the surface. Secular life receives a value of its own, and Divine grace, which in former days was limited to the pre-paration for a world to come, is found to have its im-mediate mission in the purifying of the present age.[2]

[1] 1 Tim. ii. 5.   [2] Titus ii. 11, 12.

It seems to me that, viewed from this standpoint, the pastoral epistles embrace two great ideas. The first is the recognition of the truth that the Church of Christ must be an incorporative body—a body whose essential bond of union shall be purity of life, and which, where that essential bond exists, shall consent to tolerate minor differences. The second is the recognition of the truth that the purity of the life itself ought to be allowed a wider sphere of operation, that it should not be narrowed down to the observance of a few ceremonies or the performance of a few religious duties, but should be permitted to range at will over the whole length and breadth of human nature. These, as it appears to me, are the distinctive features of these epistles so far as they bear on the subject of Paul's development, and I shall proceed as briefly as possible to exhibit each of them in turn.

And first. If I were asked to characterise the pastoral letters as distinguished from the other letters of St Paul, I should call them the broad-church epistles. It is here that distinctively and peculiarly the spirit of the apostle broadens into the recognition of a life which is capable of subsisting beneath theological differences. One of the most remarkable instances of this is afforded in the latest of all the epistles.[1] Heresies had been springing up within the Church of Ephesus. Two leaders of

[1] 2 Tim. ii. 17-20.

advanced thought had appeared—Hymenæus and
Philetus. With the special form of their heterodoxy
we have here nothing to do; speaking generally,
they may be described as in a very mild way the
forerunners of the mythical theory of Strauss, the
anticipators of that school which seeks to transform
the fact into the idea. Naturally, the enunciation
of such novel views had created a great commotion.
Reading between the lines, it is not difficult to see
that the orthodox party in the Church was clamour-
ing for the expulsion of the heretics, and that the
apostle was besieged with solicitations to have the
sentence of excommunication pronounced. How
does Paul act under these circumstances? Does he
enjoin his delegate, Timothy, to appease the ecclesiastical clamour by giving immediate effect to the
prayers of the faithful? Not at all; he tenders him
very different advice. He says, 'The foundation of
Christian membership is not theological but moral.
God Almighty alone can tell to what extent this
mental aberration has its root in a perversion of the
heart; man must be content to wait till the fruit
shall reveal the character of the tree: "The foundation of God standeth sure, having this seal, the Lord
knoweth them that are His. And, let every one that
nameth the name of Christ depart from iniquity."
Meantime, the Church of Christ, just by reason of
its vastness, should be free from all exclusiveness:
"In a great house there are not only vessels of gold

U

and of silver, but also of wood and of earth; and some to honour, and some to dishonour." A house whose position is not established may insist on admitting nothing which is not golden, or, at the very least, silver; but an institution which has made its mark can afford to let in the wood and earth also. The Church should be distinguished from the world not by its narrowness but by its power of incorporation. It should have a place not merely for the vessels of honour but for the vessels of dishonour too—a place for those commonplace minds which have been unable as yet to rise into the full recognition of truth, and whose duties must meantime be limited to the hewing of wood and the drawing of water.'

Such is the broadly tolerant expression of religious thought with which Paul closes his apostolical career, and it runs like a thread of gold through all the pastoral letters. If a man wishes to call himself by the name of Christ, Paul will give him that name; he will allow the epithet of Christian to be borne by any one who claims it. Whether that claim be well or ill founded he will leave to be determined by another tribunal, but he insists that this tribunal shall be the life and not the presbytery. He will not have the character of the tree prejudged by the seeming frailty of its branches: to speak without metaphor, he will not have a man expelled from Church membership by the apparent incongruity of his creed with interpretations previously given. He will wait for the future to tell whether the professing Christian be a real Christian ; by his fruits shall he be known. If his subsequent life be a departure from iniquity, Paul shall decide that his foundation was sure; if his subsequent life shall belie his profession, Paul shall decide that his profession was but a name. Meantime, Paul shall believe for him the best, shall assume the existence of the coming fruit, shall hope all things. He tells Timothy in the very opening of his episcopal charge that the Alpha and the Omega of that charge is charity.[1] He tells him, and he tells the world, that the end of all his development, the completion of all his ripeness, has been the perfected revelation of Christ's long-suffering patience.[2] As the night draws on, the brightest gem in the Messiah's crown has become to him its attribute most human. In the morning his eye had rested on the power of the Lord from heaven; in the evening his gaze is fixed on that restraint of power which constitutes the glory of the man Christ Jesus.

And yet, we are far from having exhausted the breadth of that humanitarian sympathy which makes the light of Paul's evening time. He has been telling Timothy to be very slow in expelling from the membership of Christ; he reminds him that in one sense, in a very deep sense, such expulsion is impossible. We have seen how in the first Roman

[1] 1 Tim. i. 5. [2] 1 Tim. i. 16.

captivity the mind of the apostle had been stirred by
the thought that there was an outer as well as an
inner membership in the body of Christ, that He
was not only the head of those who circled round
the communion-table but the head of all principalities and powers. Here, in these final letters, the
same thought asserts itself, but with a far more pronounced emphasis and in a far more definite form.
With a boldness which is almost startling in its
directness and its unqualifiedness Paul declares of
Christ that He " is the Saviour of all men, specially
of those that believe." [1] The statement is not acci-
dental nor isolated. In his charge to Titus, in a
passage already referred to, he declares in similar
terms that there is a Divine grace which " has appeared unto all men "—a grace which has revealed
itself to the world as a world, and the burden of
whose teaching is the observance of those duties
common to the day and hour. Can any one fail to
perceive in such language the presence in Paul's
mind of the thought that Christianity has exerted
an influence even over those who have not accepted
it ? He looks abroad upon the world of his day ;
it is still for the most part a pagan world. But it
is no longer the paganism of yesterday. It has not
yet received the light, but it has caught the heat.
The spirit of the new religion is in the air, and with
a subtle influence it has begun to work underground.

[1] 1 Tim. iv. 10.

The atmosphere of the Cæsars has been impregnated with the atmosphere of the Messiah. Unconsciously to themselves, men have turned the corner and are moving on a higher plane. The spirit of the new faith has run in advance of the faith itself. Christianity has penetrated into the secular institutions of the empire and imparted to them a fresh glow. Just as the sense of life in the individual precedes the exercise of vision, so in the pagan world the feeling of a new vitality had come in advance of the power to perceive its cause; like John the Baptist in the wilderness, it had gone forth as the forerunner to prepare the way of the Lord.

This was what Paul saw in his old age. He was inclined to say of Christianity what the Psalmist had said of God, " Whither can I flee from Thy presence." He felt that, however much a man might be expelled from the inner membership of Christ, it was no longer possible to put him beyond the range of Christ's outer influence. The outer influence of Christ had become Roman, and therefore potentially it had become universal. It had impregnated the breath of the world. It had come into contact with institutions which had been reared for the support of paganism, and it was exerting already a power even over lives which professed to oppose it. It was a view of this fact which prompted Paul to say that Christ was in one sense the Saviour of all men. He had received gifts even for the rebellious, and the

outer court of the tabernacle had caught a glow from
the fire of the inner sanctuary. It may be, I think
it highly probable, that the eye of the apostle saw
the vision nearer than it was in reality. Old man
as he was, he had, like the dying Moses, the spirit
of youth in him, and the spirit of youth always
sees the end already at the door. Doubtless to the
imagination of Paul the process of Christian civilisation was accelerated, doubtless he expected it to be
more rapid than it actually proved. The value of
his utterance is not the statement of a historical
fact but the revelation of a moral charity. As a
Jew, he had been able to see only two sides of the
question—to be or not to be; as a Christian, with
ever-increasing intensity there had come to him the
perception of a third and middle way — the stage
of becoming. He stood in old age on the bank of
the river, and between him and the other shore he
watched the waters roll. He saw as yet no intervening bridge of doctrine by which the two banks
could be united. But he felt that light could cross
the river independently of any bridge, and that the
men on the other side could be united by a common
life even while they were separated by a diverse
doctrine. Therefore it was that he stretched forth
a hand of fellowship into the outer court. He had
realised the fact that the new light which had risen
must sooner or later exert an elevating influence
even over those forms which had been constructed

in the night, and in the view of this prospect he was not afraid already to say of Christ, "He is the Saviour of all men."

I come now to the second of those characteristics which seem to me to mark the pastoral epistles. The first was the recognition of the truth that the Christian life is more than the Christian system; the second consists in a broader view of the Christian life itself. Not only is the influence of Christianity seen extending to the outer court, but within its own inner court there is observed a process of enlargement. Nowhere is Judaism so thoroughly transcended as in these last letters, nowhere does the type of Christian practice so completely outrun the type of Old Testament morality. Judaism had sought to make men virtuous by putting a label upon the different acts of life, by writing on this "good" and on that "bad." Into the centre of this morality Paul sends a thunderbolt. He declares that it is impossible to reach morality by means of a label, that the same act may be good to-day and bad to-morrow, that the motive of the life alone determines the worth or worthlessness of what we do. He declares that, if a man be a Christian, he can tear down the labels of prohibition, can claim the right, without trespassing, to tread in every field,—" unto the pure all things are pure." [1] It is no longer a question of what we shall do or where we shall go,

[1] Titus i. 15.

but of why we shall do and how we shall go. The act is to be determined by its motive, and according to its motive its label is to be. The Church and the world are no longer to be separated by a line which is geographical; the geographical lines are to be obliterated, and the spiritual boundary is alone to rule. The man who in the secular world manifests the Christian principle, is to be recognised as performing a deed of sacred service. Every moral act is to be esteemed a religious act, every honest day a Sabbath-day, every place of duty a place of worship, every work for man a work for God.

Accordingly, it will not surprise us to find that in these pastoral epistles Paul's first spirit of asceticism is almost extinct. It is no longer the same man who stood in the deserts of Arabia and sought to realise the presence of God alone. It is a man who has exchanged the desert for the city, and who has replaced the cares of the individual soul with the cares of the struggling multitude. As we read these letters of his old age we are impressed at every turn by the sharp point of the contrast. In the solitudes of Arabia he had seen none but God; in the streets of licentious Corinth he had separated himself from the world; in the heart of metropolitan Rome he appropriates the world as his own. It is true that he had told the Colossians to set their affections upon heavenly as distinguished from earthly things; but he had told them before this that the larger measure

of the things which they had attributed to the earth
were really the things of heaven, that Christ was the
head of all principalities and powers.   Here, in these
latest letters, almost the last trace of asceticism disappears, and the world is at once possessed and sanctified in the words, "Every creature of God is good,
and nothing to be refused." [1]   Here, in nearly every
sentence, the reader is confronted by the opposite
side of that problem which had dominated his earlier
days; it is no longer the defence of the spirit against
the encroachments of the flesh, but the vindication
of the flesh against the intolerance of the spirit.   In
Arabia, by his own admission, he had "conferred not
with flesh and blood"; in Corinth he had borne this
testimony to his spiritual need, "I keep my body
under"; in the latest stage of all he declares that
such a need has been removed and that the power
of asceticism has yielded to a higher power, "the
exercise of bodily restraint is of little advantage; [2]
but godliness is profitable for all things, having promise of the life which now is, and of that which is
to come."   He wants a religion which shall beautify
not only the prospect of heaven but the objects of
earth, which shall invest with glory not merely the
thought of a world to come but the common life of
every day and hour.   He feels that such a religion
must not be one which perpetually forbids, which

[1] 1 Tim. iv. 4.
[2] This is the real meaning of 1 Tim. iv. 8.

ever says "thou shalt not." It must be a positive
and not a negative principle, an impelling and not a
restraining force, a power which moves the world
not by the mere abstinence of the body but mainly
and pre-eminently by the joy of the soul.

But perhaps the sharpest point of contrast between Paul's earlier and later experience is to be
found in his attitude towards marriage. As we have
said, his attitude towards marriage was at no time
antagonistic; yet his feeling regarding it exhibits a
progress from negative toleration to positive favour.
He tells the Corinthians that marriage, although not
unlawful, is yet a state of fleshly tribulation from
which man and woman would do well to be free.
He tells the Ephesians that marriage, when once
contracted, is a sacramental state in which the living
sacrifice of the great Head of the Church is repeated
and mirrored in the world. He tells Timothy that
for the life of a young woman marriage is in his
opinion the most desirable goal,[1] and that the man
who makes it a subject of prohibition is to be
esteemed a heretic and a schismatic.[2] In all this
there is contrast but no contradiction. The first
voice is different from the last, but each is a true
voice and beautiful in its time. The voices are not
addressed to the same world. The first voice was
addressed to the world which preceded the second
advent; the second was spoken to an age in which

[1] 1 Tim. v. 14.   [2] 1 Tim. iv. 3.

the second advent had begun to dawn. When Paul came to Rome he felt that his coming was the beginning of Christ's coming. He felt that a new hour had struck in the history of mankind, and that he himself was designed at once to inaugurate and proclaim it. In bringing Christianity into the metropolis of the world he was really bringing Christ into the world, and to bring Christ into the world was to make all things new. The commands which served for an age outside the gospel influence were no longer applicable to a generation which had been touched by the sacred fire. It was one thing to contemplate the life of common day while yet the headship of Christ was seen only in its relation to a body of believers; it was another thing to contemplate it when He appeared as the head of all principalities and powers. In the first instance the life of common day was a life which had no significance and no glory; it was not worth preserving; it simply stood in the way. But when Christ appeared as the head even of this commonplace secular world, it received to the eye of Paul an immeasurable value. It was to him no longer the old world; it was already the scene of the second advent. So far from existing in order to vanish, it had in it an element of permanence. It was not only worth preserving, but its preservation was the main duty of man. All that ministered to its continuance became henceforth an object of interest. The marriage tie, the family rela-

tion, the social intercourse of man with man, the
progress of civilisation, the diffusion of knowledge,
the spread of commerce, the interchange of brotherhood from land to land, became in the light of the
broader revelation the opening of so many gates for
the advance of the kingdom of God.

In this new *régime*, what made the marriage tie to
Paul specially sacred was a desire to preserve inviolate the sanctity of home. He desired to preserve
that sanctity inviolate not only against the attacks
of wickedness, but mainly in these epistles against
the encroachments of what used to be deemed the
only goodness. The sun of fortune had begun to
rise on Christianity. The very fact that recently
it had been honoured by a state persecution, showed
that it was no longer an object of mere contempt.
It was beginning to make itself felt as a worldly
influence—as a factor which must be reckoned with
in estimating the strength of the empire. If, for
those inside its pale, this growing importance was
in one sense an advantage, it was in another sense
fraught with danger. The fear in former days was
that the allurements of the world might seduce the
Christian from the service of the Church; the fear
in Paul's mind at this later time was that the attrac-
tions of the Church might draw away the Christian
from the legitimate service of the world. He was
afraid that the increasing popularity of this new
mode of life might lead its votaries to sink the

citizen in the devotee, to neglect the common cares and duties of the hour for the uncommon cares and duties of the inner sanctuary. It was a sense of this danger which prompted Paul in his old age to stand forth as the protector of the fireside, the guardian of the domestic altar. If in the spring-time he had seen the world chiefly in its aspects antagonistic to religion, he amply redeemed himself in the autumn of his days. He came forth as the champion of a secular religiousness, of a service of God which might be given within the walls of an ordinary dwelling. Every note of his latest writings is pervaded by this spirit of secular guardianship—this desire to preserve for its own sake the life of the family and the household. There were hundreds of young men who thought it incumbent on them to desert their domestic duties for the duties of the missionary; Paul says, " If any widow have children or nephews, let them learn first to show piety at home, and to requite their parents." [1] There were men who sacrificed the comforts of the family to the claims of Christian liberality; Paul says, " If any provide not for his own, and specially for those of his own house, he hath denied the faith, and is worse than an infidel." [2] There were domestic servants who, on the ground of their Christian profession, laid claim to a social equality with their masters, assumed that the republicanism in the sight

[1] 1 Tim. v. 4.   [2] 1 Tim. v. 8.

of God abolished all distinctions in the grades of man; Paul says, " They that have believing masters, let them not despise them, because they are brethren ; but rather do them service, because they are faithful and beloved." [1]

Such is the tenor of these pastoral epistles. They are a defence of the secular against the encroachments of the sacred—a vindication of the essential sanctity of the natural rights of man. I cannot but remark how, when viewed in this light, these epistles acquire an entirely new significance. It has been no uncommon thing from a literary point of view to speak of them with disparagement. Even those who have accepted their genuineness have been willing to concede that they indicate a drooping in the apostle's wing. They tell us that there is a marked contrast between the sublime fire which flashes from the apostle's eye in the letter to Galatia, and the homely touch of the hand which is laid on the heads of Timothy and Titus. And so, doubtless, there is ; but I would rather call it home-like than homely. In the reading of these later epistles we feel that we are no longer breathing mountain-air ; yet, if we read them aright, we shall find that we have exchanged the mountain-air for the atmosphere of a more useful environment. We have left the dizzy heights of speculation where the mind dwelt on those transcendental problems in which the spirit

[1] 1 Tim. vi. 2.

of man contemplates his relation to eternity. But if in abandoning these heights we have lost something in elevation, we have gained something in breadth. We have descended into a plain which is more prosaic, but which is at the same time more human. The pastoral epistles are home-like simply because their subject is home. If they exhibit a drooping of the wing, it is because they have discovered a region lying beneath the ordinary flight of religion. They have discovered that there belongs to Christianity a world which was once thought to belong to Satan—the world of home-life, the world of the family altar, the world of common secular toil. It is not their greater poverty but their superior riches which makes them prosaic; they are less filled with the transcendental because they are more full of man.

I confess, indeed, that the order of Paul's experience is here very different from the order of common experience. In the lives of men in general the objects of the outer world lose somewhat of their magnitude as the shadows of old age deepen. Apart altogether from religion, the tendency of advancing years is to deprive the incidents of common day of much of that absorbing interest which constituted their dominion over the years of manhood. But Paul's experience is entirely the reverse. He is perfectly conscious, indeed, that the snows of age are falling round him; he says so in the epistle to

Philemon. But the peculiarity of his case is that the objects of life become interesting just in proportion to the deepening of the snow. The time of his manhood had not been a time of much interest in the present world. He had stood then upon Mount Nebo and gazed into the prospect of the promised land; his eye was indeed undimmed, yet his natural strength had been abated. The vision of the heavenly Canaan had to some extent paralysed the force of his human nature, and the sight of the Delectable Mountains had dwarfed his view of the plain. But here, standing in the twilight, the picture is reversed. At the approach of night the forms of this world's life for the first time fully and freely emerge upon his gaze. The noonday of manhood had suppressed them, the fire of youthful enthusiasm had hid them; but the shadows of old age revealed them in all their possibility and power. The time of Paul's declining earthly day is precisely the time when the earth to him acquires its full significance; in relation to this world the saying was in him fulfilled, "at evening-time it shall be light."

And the explanation of all this we have seen. It is no accident, no freak of history; it is in strict consistency with the whole order of Paul's development. If the widening of his worldly views at the approach of old age is a somewhat abnormal experience, it is because his conversion to Christianity was itself in its method abnormal. The other leaders of

the new religion began, as we have seen, at the base
of the triangle and gradually climbed up to its apex;
Paul began at the apex and gradually descended to
the base. The other leaders received Christianity
at first in its most human and worldly aspect; they
came to the Son of man for the sake of that earthly
bread which was broken by His hand. But Paul
received his first knowledge of Christ at the top of
the triangle. He caught his earliest vision of Him
not as the Son of man but as the Son of God. His
eye rested at the beginning on no Galilean plains,
on no image of a human form. It rested on a form
which had freed itself from the limitations of humanity, which had clothed itself in a superhuman garb.
He had begun with the Christ of resurrection; he
had started on the heights. It was inevitable that
any future development must be a progress downward. It was inevitable that just in proportion as
he descended from the height he must reach the
breadth of Christianity. The base of the triangle
which to his brother apostles was the starting-point
was to him the goal. Every stage of his journey
was necessarily a stage nearer to the human, nearer
to the world of common day. Throughout the
course of these pages we have been trying to trace
these steps of descent. We have been seeking to
indicate that process of gradual broadening which
marked the advance of his spiritual life from its
apex amid the mountains of Arabia to its base in

the heart of the great metropolis. We have endeavoured to distinguish those successive stages of experience by which he approached ever nearer to a
sympathy with man as man. And we have found
that with him the breadth has grown in proportion
to the descent. The moment furthest removed from
transcendentalism has been the moment most incorporative of the world; the writings least full of
systematic theology have been the epistles most
filled with man. In Arabia he stood at the highest
summit of heavenly vision, but the deepest ground
of earthly sympathy was found only in Rome.

There we shall leave him—leave him amid those
shadows which brought to him his fullest, latest
light. The shades of night were gathering round
him; the walls of the prison-house had finally en-
closed him; the infirmities of old age had begun to
tell on his physical frame. Yet neither the age nor
the captivity nor the final martyrdom constitutes
the fitting close of such a life as his; its fitting close
is its latest breadth of sympathy. It is here that
one comes to understand what has often been a
puzzle to historians—why the writer of the Acts,
after having brought Paul almost to the gates of
martyrdom, should have ended his narrative by
leaving him unharmed before the gates. The reason
lies in the writer's sense of the true situation. He
knew that the hour of Paul's tragedy was at the
same time the hour of his triumph, and the tragedy

to his mind was lost in the triumph. He knew that
Paul was never so great, never so powerful, never
so instrumental to the common-weal, as when he
stood amid the declining light and claimed the world
for Christ. It furnished to him that climax for his
book which he had contemplated from its very beginning. " Ye shall be witnesses unto me both in
Jerusalem, and in all Judea, and in Samaria, and
unto the uttermost part of the earth,"[1] are the words
in which he expresses its prefatory plan. It is a
triangular plan; it follows the course of Christianity
from its narrowest point to its broadest base. Jerusalem, Judea, Samaria, the far-off parts of the West
where stood the great metropolis of the world,—these
were the gradations through which the earliest of
Church historians proposed to trace Christianity's
progress. Each stage was an expansion, each step
was a step nearer to man. He beheld the new
religion passing from its narrowest precincts within
the walls of Jerusalem into the wider atmosphere of
the surrounding Judaic district. He beheld it thence
overleaping the walls of orthodox Judaism itself and
entering into that region of Samaria which had been
long to the Jew a proscribed land. He beheld it,
lastly, transcending altogether the limits of Palestine
and penetrating with the footsteps of Paul into
the very heart of secular paganism. When he had
arrived at that climax he felt it time to lay down

[1] Acts i. 8.

his pen. He felt that when the apostle had reached the interior of the great metropolis he had reached the beginning of the end, had seen the inauguration of Christianity's triumph ; and that here, accordingly, the curtain ought to fall. We too may be content in imitation of so illustrious an example to let the vision of the triumph eclipse the scene of the martyrdom, and to leave the missionary of the Gentiles in the field of his undying glory.

THE END.

PRINTED BY WILLIAM BLACKWOOD AND SONS.

DATE DUE

JUL 1 1994	
APR 1 1995	
MAR 3 0 1995	
GAYLORD	PRINTED IN U.S.A.